Pastoral and Occasional Liturgies

A COWLEY PUBLICATIONS BOOK

ROWMAN & LITTLEFIELD PUBLISHERS, INC.

Published in the United States of America
by Rowman & Littlefield Publishers, Inc.
A wholly owned subsidiary of The Rowman & Littlefield Publishing Group, Inc.
4501 Forbes Boulevard, Suite 200, Lanham, Maryland 20706
www.rowmanlittlefield.com

Estover Road
Plymouth PL6 7PY
United Kingdom

Copyright © 1998 Leonel L. Mitchell
First Rowman & Littlefield edition 2007

British Library Cataloguing in Publication Information Available

Library of Congress Cataloging-in-Publication Data

Mitchell, Leonel L. (Leonel Lake), 1930–
  Pastoral and occasional liturgies: a ceremonial guide/Leonel L. Mitchell
      p.   cm.
  Includes bibliographic references.
  ISBN-13: 978-1-56101-158-2 (pbk. : alk. paper)
  ISBN-10: 1-56101-158-4 (pbk. : alk. paper)
   1. Occasional services—Texts—History and criticism. 2. Episcopal Church. Book of
common prayer (1979). 3. Episcopal Church. Book of occasional services. 4. Episcopal
Church—Liturgy. 5. Anglican Communion—United States—Liturgy. I. Title.
BX5947.025M58 1998
264'.035—dc21   98-18656
                                                                  CIP

Printed in the United States of America.

♾™ The paper used in this publication meets the minimum requirements of
American National Standard for Information Sciences—Permanence of
Paper for Printed Library Materials, ANSI/NISO Z39.48-1992.

Table of Contents

Preface xi

Chapter One
The Daily Offices   page 1

1. The Offices as Daily Devotions 5

2. Liturgical Celebration of the Office 6
   A. Ceremonial at the Office 6
   B. Vesture for the Office 8
   C. Music at the Office 9
      a. Singing Psalms and Canticles 9
      b. Other Music in the Office 10
      c. Hymns and Anthems at the Office 11

3. Celebrating Morning Prayer 12
   A. Daily Celebration 12
      a. Opening of the Office 12
      b. Invitatory and Psalms 13
      c. Readings and Canticles 14
      d. Creed, Suffrages, and Collects 15
      e. Anthem, Hymn, and Intercessions 16
   B. Sunday and Holy Day Celebration 17
   C. Morning Prayer as the Eucharistic Word Liturgy 18

4. Celebrating Evensong 20
   A. Daily Celebration 20
      a. Lucernarium 20
      b. The Psalms 22
      c. The Lessons and Canticles 22
      d. Creed, Suffrages, and Collects 23
      e. Anthem, Hymn, and Close of Office 24
   B. Solemn Evensong 25
   C. An Order of Worship for the Evening 26

5. Noonday Prayer and Compline 27
   A. Celebrating An Order of Service for Noonday 27
   B. Celebrating Compline 29

6. Vigil of the Resurrection 30

Chapter Two
Proper Seasonal Liturgies   **page 32**

1. Lessons and Carols 32
   A. Advent Festival of Lessons and Music 33
   B. Christmas Festival of Lessons and Music 34

2. Blessing of the Creche 35

3. Service for New Year's Eve 36

4. Candlemas Procession 38

5. The Rogation Procession 40
   A. The Procession Before a Rogation Day Eucharist 41
   B. The Procession Apart from the Eucharist 43

6. The Baptismal Feasts 43
   A. Baptismal Vigils. 44
      a. Vigil for the Eve of the Baptism of Our Lord 44
      b. Vigil for the Eve of All Saints' Day 45
      c. Vigil on the Eve of Baptism 45
   B. The Renewal of Baptismal Vows 46

Chapter Three
Pastoral Offices

page 48

1. Rites Related to Christian Initiation 48
   A. Emergency Baptism 48
   B. Admission of Catechumens 49
   C. Welcoming Returning Members and
   Members Baptized in Other Traditions 50
   D. Confirmation, Reception, and Reaffirmation 51
   E. The Preparation of Parents and Godparents
   for the Baptism of Infants and Young Children 53
      a. The Blessing of Parents at the Beginning of the Pregnancy 53
      b. Thanksgiving for the Birth or Adoption of a Child 54
      c. Holy Baptism 54
      d. Adaptation for Special Circumstances 55

2. Marriage Rites 55
   A. The Celebration and Blessing of a Marriage 57
      a. Entrance Procession 58
      b. The Declaration of Consent 59
      c. The Ministry of the Word 60
      d. The Marriage 60
      e. The Blessing of the Marriage 62
      f. The Nuptial Eucharist 62
      g. The Exit 63
      h. Weddings at the Sunday Eucharist 64
   B. The Blessing of a Civil Marriage 64
   C. Anniversary of a Marriage 65

3. Reconciliation of a Penitent 66
    A. Form One. 69
    B. Form Two 69
    C. Lay Confessors 70

4. Christian Service. 71
    A. A Form of Commitment to Christian Service 72
    B. Commissioning for Lay Ministries in the Church 72

5. Celebration for a Home 74
    A. The Full Service 74
    B. A Shorter Version 76

6. Ministry to the Sick and Dying. 76
    A. Ministration to the Sick 77
        a. Ministry of the Word 77
        b. Special Confession 78
        c. Laying on of Hands and Anointing 78
        d. Holy Communion. 79
            i. Eucharist in the Sick Room 80
            ii. Communion from the Reserved Sacrament. 81
            iii. Distribution of Communion by Lay Eucharistic Ministers 83
    B. A Public Service of Healing. 85
    C. Ministration at the Time of Death 87

7. The Burial of the Dead. 88
    A. The Vigil or Wake. 90
    B. Reception of the Body 91
    C. Burial of the Dead: Rite Two. 91
        a. Entrance Rite 92
        b. Ministry of the Word 93
        c. The Homily 93
        d. The Prayers of the People 94
        e. At the Eucharist. 94
        f. The Commendation 95
        g. The Procession from the Church 96
        h. The Committal 96

    D. Burial of the Dead: Rite One. 98

    E. Funerals Without the Eucharist 98

    F. Funerals Without a Priest. 99

    G. An Order for Burial 99

    H. Burial of One Who Does Not Profess the Christian Faith 100

    I. Funerals in Houses or Funeral Homes 101

    J. Funerals Without a Body or Ashes 102

    K. Memorial Services. 102

Chapter Four

Episcopal Services **page 104**

1. The Bishop in the Parish Liturgy 106

2. Celebration of a New Ministry 107

    A. For Instituting a Rector 107

    B. A Deputy as Institutor 111

    C. The Inauguration of Other Ministries 111

    D. Installation of Ministry Teams 113

3. Consecration of Churches 113

    A. Consecration of a New Church. 113

        a. Entrance Procession. 114

        b. Prayer of Consecration 115

        c. Blessing of the Font (and Baptism) 116

        d. Dedication of Lectern and Pulpit. 116

        e. Liturgy of the Word 117

        f. Dedication of the Organ. 117

        g. Gospel and Sermon 117

        h. Other Pastoral Offices. 117

        i. Prayers of the People. 117

        j. Consecration of the Altar 118

        k. The Eucharist 118

    B. For a Church or Chapel Long in Use 119

    C. The Dedication of Church Furnishings. 119

4. Ordination Rites 119
   A. The Ordination of Priests and Deacons 120
   B. The Ordination of Bishops 121
     a. The Entrance and Presentation 122
     b. The Ministry of the Word 123
     c. The Examination 123
     d. The Consecration of the Bishop 124
     e. The Eucharist 125
   C. Recognition and Investiture of a Diocesan Bishop 126
     a. The Recognition 126
     b. The Investiture 127
     c. The Seating 128
     d. The Eucharist 128
   D. Welcoming and Seating of a Bishop in the Cathedral 129

Chapter Five

Liturgical Resources   **page 130**

Preface

This is the third and final volume of a series intended to assist all who bear responsibility for the planning and conduct of public worship in the Episcopal Church in that task. The first volume of the series, *The Ceremonies of the Eucharist: A Guide to Celebration*, was written by the late Howard E. Galley. I wrote the second, *Lent, Holy Week, Easter, and the Great Fifty Days: A Ceremonial Guide*. Material covered in the first two volumes is generally not repeated in this one, and like the previous volumes, the presumed setting for the services described remains medium-sized Episcopal churches, with the obvious exception of the services relating to the ordination and installation of bishops, which will usually take place in cathedrals or in other large assembly spaces.

The first section of this volume deals with the celebration of the daily offices. The second describes those seasonal liturgies that are not included in the Lent-Easter cycle; most are from *The Book of Occasional Services*. The third section includes pastoral services from both *The Book of Common Prayer* and *The Book of Occasional Services*, including catechumenal rites, the Reconciliation of a Penitent, healing services, and the blessing of homes. The final section deals with episcopal rites.

It is important to remember that there is no one "correct" way to celebrate the rites of the church, although there are some very bad ways. In commenting on the role of those who plan and lead these celebrations Marion Hatchett said it well: "The minister is not a magician but a liturgical functionary, left free to determine what ceremonies might be most appropriate in particular circumstances and with particular rites or texts."[1] Liturgy arises out of the interaction of the congregation with one another, with the liturgical text, and with God. It is conditioned both by the space in which it is celebrated and by the cultural norms of the participants. Clearly, services like the Consecration of a Church need to be adapted to the space that is being consecrated, and considerations such as the size of the sanctuary will (or at least should) affect the way in which all services are planned and conducted. Equally clearly, weddings and funerals are particularly influenced by cultural norms. But the building and cultural norms influence all liturgy, and every congregation has its own liturgical and musical traditions. Our liturgy needs to be *ours*, and not a copy of the liturgy of another congregation. Yet a guide to a reasonable, consistent plan for celebration is extremely valuable.

The books in this series are best read with a pencil in hand, making notes over the years to adapt what is written here to your own specific situation. A pencil, rather than a pen, will make it easy to revise the notes for the next time on the basis of your own experience.

I am acutely aware that my experience with episcopal services is limited and derivative, and I am most grateful to the Rt. Rev. Henry I. Louttit, Bishop of Georgia, and the Rt. Rev. Paul V. Marshall, Bishop of Bethlehem, for reading the draft of that section and making helpful suggestions and comments.

Finally, I wish to extend my deepest gratitude and thanks to my own teacher, the Rev. Canon H. Boone Porter, sometime Professor of Liturgics at The General Theological Seminary and editor of *The Living Church*, for a lifetime ministry of teaching in classroom, church, and the natural world. He taught me much of what I know about the liturgy, but most important of all, he taught me how to find out what I did not know. I am ever in his debt.

Leonel L. Mitchell
The Baptism of Our Lord 1998

---

1. Marion J. Hatchett, *A Manual of Ceremonial for the New Prayer Book* (Sewanee: St. Luke's Journal of Theology, 1977), 1.

Chapter One

The Daily Offices

Before we can examine the celebration of the daily offices, we need to consider what the offices are and what they are intended to do. *The Book of Common Prayer* simply takes the existence and importance of the office for granted and sets forth daily Morning and Evening Prayer as "regular services appointed for public worship in this Church" (BCP 13) without giving any rationale or theological justification for this practice.

Daily prayer, both private and corporate, has been a part of Christian tradition from apostolic times and has its roots in Jewish practice. Observant Jews recited the *Shema* found in the sixth chapter of Deuteronomy—"Hear, O Israel: The LORD is our God, the LORD alone. You shall love the LORD your God..."— morning and evening, and its recitation formed the central core of daily synagogue worship. It is this tradition of daily prayer that passed into early Christianity. In the fourth century, when it became possible for Christians to worship publicly, the corporate celebration of morning and evening prayer became widespread. As Robert Taft has pointed out in *The Liturgy of the Hours in East and West*, considered by many to be the definitive contemporary work on the daily offices:

> Per se there is no special mystical significance about morning and evening as times of prayer. They are the beginning and end of the day, and so it was perfectly natural to select them as the "symbolic moments" in which we express what ought to be the quality of the whole day.[1]

---

1.   Robert Taft, *The Liturgy of the Hours in East and West* (Collegeville: Liturgical Press, 1986), 358.

Yet for Christians the daily offices have always been more than convenient times to pray. Frère Max Thurian of Taizé has characterized them as "a part of the praise which the whole creation offered to its creator." For Christians this praise is offered in union with Jesus Christ, our great High Priest, who continually offers the praise and intercession of the church with the memorial of his sacrifice (Hebrews 7:24-25). Thurian notes:

> In the communion of saints, all Christians pray with Christ and in him. The liturgy of the Church, the Daily Office, is part of the heavenly liturgy, of the office of Christ and the angels, presenting before the throne of the Father the prayers of the saints, together with their own praise and intercession.[2]

The content of the office is remembrance (*anamnesis*), praise and thanksgiving, which flow into petition and intercession. The morning office dedicates the new day to God, and the evening office at the close of day leads us to reflect on the hours just passed, with thanksgiving for the good they have brought and sorrow for the evil we have done. Light is, of course, the basic natural symbol behind the celebration of the office, and for Christians it is "the light of Christ." The sunrise in the morning is a powerful symbol of the rising Sun of Righteousness (Malachi 4:2), and the "vesper light" shining in the evening brings Christians to the worship of the light that "shines in the darkness" (John 1:4-5). In Taft's words,

> All of creation is a cosmic sacrament of our saving God, and the Church's use of such symbolism in the office is but a step in the restoration of all things in Christ (Eph. 1:10). For the Christian everything, including the day and the night, the sun and its setting, can be a means of communication with God. "The heavens declare the glory of God and the firmament proclaims his handiwork" (Ps. 18[19]:1).[3]

The office, then, is liturgy, and its principal content—the event it celebrates—is the paschal mystery of the dying and rising of Jesus Christ, and our participation therein. This is the central core of baptism, of the eucharist, of the Lord's Day, of Easter, and of the office as well. It is our

---

2. Max Thurian, *The Taizé Office* (London: Faith Press, 1966), 9, 11.

3. Taft, *Liturgy of the Hours*, 348.

priestly work as the people of God in proclaiming the paschal mystery. "The daily office in particular," Max Thurian reminds us, "belongs to the common exercise of the royal priesthood of all who are baptized."[4]

Yet in spite of this theological rationale, a problem remains. As John Crichton has aptly commented, "The Church holds a high doctrine of the Divine Office, yet its practice must be said to be low."[5] W. Jardine Grisbrooke has stated the problem as succinctly as possible:

> There appears to be a not inconsiderable number of worshipers who do not frequent services other than the eucharist because they do not find the actual form of these services offered to them to be satisfying—often without knowing exactly why not. People in this category with whom I have discussed the subject do not appear to want a less formal, less liturgical type of service; on the contrary, they appear to want liturgical forms more consonant with their experience at the eucharist than are the existing forms of the office available to them.[6]

Grisbrooke is unquestionably right. Many clergy who have attempted to introduce the daily offices into their parish worship have found a profound lack of interest on the part of most lay people. Some of this may be the result of human apathy or the pace of contemporary society, which makes it difficult to assemble people for any purpose, but the root cause is that the daily offices are not *celebrated*. Because they are simply recited or sung, people do not experience the office as liturgy. Recited offices are seen not as corporate worship but as a group of individuals at prayer, and many people, both clergy and laity, find private recitation at least as spiritually satisfying, if not more. Choral offices are often seen primarily as choir concerts, and if the music is good, will attract an audience for occasional performances but will not create a community at prayer.

The origin of the problem lies deep in the history of the office, and there is no "quick fix" that will send Christians trooping to daily Morning Prayer. Historically, there are two forms of the office that have interacted and

---

4. Thurian, *Taizé Office*, 10.

5. John D. Crichton, *The Church's Worship* (New York: Sheed & Ward, 1964), 187.

6. W. Jardine Grisbrooke, "A Contemporary Liturgical Problem: The Divine Office and Public Worship," *Studia Liturgica* 8 (1971-1972), 130. Grisbrooke's article appears in three issues of *Studia Liturgica* (8 [1971-1972], 129-68; 9 [1973], 3-18, 81-106).

produced many hybrid offspring. The daily prayer of the early Christians was formalized in the fourth and fifth centuries, when the church emerged from the persecutions, as the *cathedral office*. This does not mean choral evensong as celebrated in Anglican cathedrals, but morning and evening prayer as they were celebrated by the ecclesiastical community in the great churches of the Roman world. The cathedral office made use of a small number of psalms, hymns, and canticles, sometimes a scripture reading chosen for its appropriateness, and congregational prayer similar to the eucharistic prayers of the people. William Storey, who was largely responsible for instituting the celebration of a cathedral office at the University of Notre Dame in the 1970s, described these offices as

> almost exclusively worship (*latreia*) for its own sake: praise, thanksgiving, adoration, petition...stylistically as reasonably brief, colorful, ceremonious, odiforous, and full of movement...very churchy, somewhat vulgar, clergy-dominated and impossibly simple to participate in.[7]

The pure form of the *monastic office,* as it developed in Egyptian monasticism, on the other hand, was basically a scheme for corporate meditation. It was ascetic, nonceremonious, and meditative. The psalms were recited slowly by a single voice so that all might reflect on their meaning. Its organizational principles were the recitation of the entire psalter and the continuous reading of holy scripture. It followed neither the liturgical year nor the sanctoral cycle of readings. Its purpose was to fill day and night with prayer until the Lord's return in glory, so that he might find the church watching and praying (Mark 13:35-37).

All existing forms of the office are hybrids deriving from these sources. Even the Benedictine office has adopted the liturgical calendar, hymns, and corporate recitation of the psalms from the cathedral office. Western offices have, nevertheless, become extensively monasticized over the centuries, and lost many of their cathedral features, such as the evening lamp lighting. While the monastic form of the office has a great appeal to some, it is seldom popular. Its use of long narrative psalms and "unedifying" readings that happen to follow in course, as well as its lack of movement and

---

7. William Storey, "The Liturgy of the Hours: Cathedral versus Monastery," in *Christians at Prayer*, ed. John Gallen (Notre Dame: University Press, 1977), 66.

ceremony, make it unpopular. On the other hand, its non-clerical character—anyone is permitted to preside—is a strong point for contemporary use. The Order of Worship for the Evening in *The Book of Common Prayer* and the Resurrection Vigil in the Canadian *Book of Alternative Services* are attempts to provide more cathedral-type offices.

1. The Offices as Daily Devotions

The offices as we experience them today often try to be two things at once. First, they try to be daily prayer for clergy and devout laity. They may be read individually or in groups, but they are seen as personal prayer and Bible reading, a devotional exercise. Second, they try to be celebrations for the congregation. These are often difficult to combine, and we should try to be clear which is our primary intention.

Certainly the use of the daily offices as private prayer is to be encouraged. The English prayer book requires priests and deacons who do not celebrate the offices in their congregation to read them privately, and many American clergy and lay people do so as well. Those who use the offices privately should feel free to adapt them to their own needs since, in the form they appear in the prayer book, they are clearly designed for corporate use.

It is also reasonable to encourage families or other small groups to pray together using Morning Prayer, Noonday Prayer, Evening Prayer, or Compline, depending on the time of day. Such groups may even find it desirable to pray in the church or a chapel. If members of the group do not pray together every day, they may find it helpful to choose psalms and lessons that can stand alone, or to combine or lengthen some readings for continuity (see BCP 934). No special ceremonial is needed, although a group may wish to make their common prayer more of a liturgical celebration by singing hymns, burning incense, and standing, sitting, and kneeling as appropriate.

2. Liturgical Celebration of the Office

Important and desirable as the private or small group uses of the offices are, they are not their liturgical celebration. Celebrations require movement and ceremony, and when ceremony integral to the office is lacking, it is frequently supplied, as in the ceremonies often associated with Sunday Morning Prayer, such as processions with collection plates and flags. Grisbrooke has suggested that

> in the office, just as in the rest of the liturgy, the Word may be, and should be, proclaimed in act as well as in word, by significant ceremonial. Ceremonial, however simply or however elaborately it may be performed, should be envisaged as an essential and integral part of the office, if the latter is to be what any worship must be, a laying open and laying bare of the whole [person] to God's self-communication, and a response of the whole [person] to that communication....
>
> By ceremonial integral to the office I mean ceremonial which expresses and manifests the themes of the office, and which is conceived as part of the office's basic structure, not added as a decorative embellishment.[8]

A. Ceremonial at the Office

The principal theme of the office that ceremonial manifests is light. The great light ceremony is the *lucernarium*, or lamp lighting, which accompanies the hymn *Phos hilaron* at Evening Prayer. This ceremony, common to almost all forms of the office from ancient times, had dropped out of the Roman office and did not find its way into *The Book of Common Prayer* until 1979. It opens An Order of Worship for the Evening, but it may introduce Evening Prayer or an evening celebration of the eucharist (BCP 112).

There is no comparable morning ceremony. It is the rising sun that manifests the light of Christ, both in his incarnation and in his resurrection. The use of a morning hymn to the light, such as "O splendor of God's glory bright" (Hymn 5) or Charles Wesley's "Christ, whose glory fills the skies" (Hymn 6, 7) following the invitatory (*Venite* or alternative) can underscore the theme.[9]

---

8. Grisbrooke, *SL* 9, 100f., 103.

Another ceremony of the office is the morning and evening offering of incense "to give to those elements of adoration and supplication which are of the essence of the office expression in act as well as in word."[10] The use of incense is both scriptural and traditional. Psalm 141:2 ("Let my prayer be set forth in your sight as incense, the lifting up of my hands as the evening sacrifice") is traditionally associated with evensong; Malachi 1:11 ("For from the rising of the sun to its setting my name is great among the nations, and in every place incense is offered to my name, and a pure offering") is often cited by the church fathers as testifying to the universality of Christian worship; and Revelation 5:8 and 8:3-4 identify incense with "the prayers of the saints."

The Book of Common Prayer says that incense "is appropriate after the candles have been lighted [in the *lucernarium*] and while the hymn *Phos hilaron* is being sung" (BCP 143). In the Byzantine tradition incense is offered during the prayers, and this can appropriately be done by Anglicans as well. Incense may also be offered during the gospel canticles (*Benedictus* and *Magnificat*) and at the reading of the gospel.

The incense need not be carried in a thurible and used to cense people and objects. It can be burned in a standing incense burner in the sanctuary where it can be smelled and its rising smoke seen by the congregation. One extremely effective use of incense with a small congregation is to burn it in a standing incense burner in the middle of the assembly, and during the prayers to encourage those offering petitions to add a grain of incense to the fire, giving ceremonial expression to the psalm verse "Let my prayer be set forth in your sight as incense" (141:2).

Grisbrooke suggests a third category of ceremonies integral to the office, those connected with the reading of scripture. "The scriptures should not simply be found lying ready on a lectern; they should be brought in in procession, with the singing of appropriate material, act and word complementing each other."[11] He recommends the use of the same

---

9. Ormonde Plater has translated some morning chants called *Praise for Creation* from the French offices published by Les Éditions de l'Abbaye de Sylvanès in Camarès, France. They were published in *OPEN* 41, no. 1-2 (Spring-Summer 1995) along with the comparable evening chants called Thanksgiving for the Light of Christ. Creative use can be made of both.

10. Grisbrooke, *SL* 9, 103.

exceptions, the method is not recommended, either for singing or recitation.

Traditionally, Anglican and plainsong (Gregorian) chants have been used to sing the psalms. Setting of the canticles for both systems are in *The Hymnal 1982* among the service music. *The Anglican Chant Psalter* and *The Plainsong Psalter* contain settings for all one hundred fifty psalms. *The Plainsong Psalter* also contains antiphons drawn from the psalms or from other passages of scripture for use with them (see BCP 141). The accompaniment edition of *The Hymnal 1982* contains additional chants in its supplement, as well as simplified Anglican chants (S 408–S 416). It also contains an index of metrical psalms (p. 679) and metrical canticles (pp. 680-681) which may be sung in place of the prose versions.

The French church musician Joseph Gelineau developed another style of chant that is widely used in Europe. Settings of his chant to English texts are available, and provide another option: *The Psalms: An Inclusive Language Version Based on the Grail Translation from the Hebrew* (Chicago: G.I.A. Publications, 1986) is the most recent English version of the Gelineau psalms. There are also many composed settings of various psalms and canticles. Examples in *The Hymnal 1982* include Jack Noble White's setting of the *Venite* (S 35), Ronald Arnatt's and McNeil Robinson's settings of "O Gracious Light" (S 60 and S 61), John Rutter's "A Song of Praise" (S 236), Arnatt's "Song of Simeon" (S 260), and Calvin Hampton's "A Song to the Lamb" (S 266), as well as numerous settings of *Gloria in excelsis* (S 272–S 281). There are others in the hymnal supplement.

The variety of choices available should make it possible for most congregations to sing the psalms and canticles when the office is celebrated. The plainsong and Gelineau settings do not require organ accompaniment. Often a good cantor can lead a congregation in responsorial psalmody or unison direct chanting.

The invitatory psalm and canticles are sung standing. Other psalms are normally sung sitting, although they may also be sung standing, especially if they are short. When the psalms are recited either posture may be assumed.

b. Other Music in the Office

The versicles and responses and the prayers may also be sung and frequently are. Music is included with the service music in *The Hymnal 1982*. The Preces (the opening versicles and responses) for Morning Prayer

(I) are at S 1 and the Suffrages (the versicles and responses before the collects) are at S 22 and S 23. The Preces for Evening Prayer (I) are at S 26 and the Suffrages at S 29 and S 30. For Morning Prayer (II) the Preces are at S 33 and the Suffrages at S 52 and S 53. For Evening Prayer (II) the Preces are at S 58 and the Suffrages at S 63 and S 64. Two tones for singing collects are in the supplement at S 447 and S 448.

The readings may also be sung, but this is less frequently done except for the short lessons at Noonday Prayer, Compline, and in the Order for Evening. The tone for short lessons is in the Appendix to *The Hymnal 1982* at S 449. The short lessons for the noonday office are at S 301–S 304, and those for Compline at S 327–S 330. The criterion for singing readings is not solemnity but proclamation. If singing enhances the proclamation of the word, then it is desirable, but if it detracts from the proclamation either by rendering the words unintelligible or by calling attention to itself, then it is not.

c. Hymns and Anthems at the Office

An office hymn is a traditional part of the celebration of the daily office. A hymn is mentioned in the rubrics of Morning and Evening Prayer after the prayer for mission, where the prayer book says, "Here may be sung a hymn or anthem" (BCP 101, 125). This is the traditional place in Anglican offices for the singing of a choir anthem, and if one is to be sung, it should be done there. If there is no choir anthem, an office hymn may be sung in its place.

Another traditional place for the office hymn at Morning Prayer is following the invitatory, before the psalms. At Evening Prayer "some other suitable hymn," which could be an office hymn, may replace the *Phos hilaron.* Office hymns which, like *Phos hilaron*, are hymns to the light, are especially suitable in this position. During Advent, for example, the office hymn "Creator of the stars at night" (Hymn 60) is particularly appropriate used in this way following the lighting of the Advent wreath. Alternatively, an evening office hymn may be sung before the *Magnificat.*

There is no reason to use only translations of medieval office hymns. Thomas Ken's hymns—"Awake, my soul, and with the sun" (Hymn 11) and "All praise to thee, my God, this night" (Hymn 43)—were written to be office hymns, and many modern hymns are equally suitable. An office hymn is not intended to be a musical interlude, but to enhance a central theme of the office: morning, noon, evening, night, light, resurrection, creation, penitence, thanksgiving, supplication, praise. Office hymns may also enhance the theme proper to a feast or season.

At the noonday office the hymn precedes the psalms, as indicated by the rubric (BCP 103), and at Compline it follows the short lesson (BCP 132). The prayer book also permits a hymn to be used in place of a canticle "in special circumstances" (BCP 142).

3. Celebrating Morning Prayer

A. Daily Celebration

Except in residential communities such as religious houses and seminaries where the community gathers daily to sing the office, daily celebrations will almost always be "small group" liturgies, in which ceremonial will be reduced and music either lacking or minimal. Where it is possible, at least the canticles and office hymn should be sung, and some ceremonial used. During conferences and retreats it will often be possible to celebrate the morning office more fully.

The altar candles are lighted. The officiant vests either in alb (and stole, if ordained) or in choir dress. The reader may enter with the officiant, carrying the Bible and placing it on the lectern. The reader may wear an alb (or cassock and surplice) or ordinary clothes. A cantor or precentor who is to lead the singing may enter with them and sit beside the officiant (or in some other convenient place). The cantor may wear an alb (or cassock and surplice). If incense is used it may be burning in a standing burner or carried in by a thurifer. If there is a vested choir, the singers may enter with the officiant, or they may take their places before the service, like other members of the congregation. The officiant goes to the presider's chair, or to an officiant's stall in the choir. In many churches officiating is most effectively done from the presider's chair, while in other churches, especially those with a large monastic-style choir, the officiant's stall in choir is preferable both for the offices and the eucharistic Word liturgy.

a. Opening of the Office

The office may begin immediately with the officiant singing (or saying) "Lord, open our lips" (BCP 80). If the confession of sin is used, the officiant recites one of the opening sentences, then faces the people and says the invitation to confession. The officiant kneels with the congregation for the confession and rises and faces the people for the absolution, making the sign of the cross at "forgive you all your sins." If the officiant is not a priest, he or she remains kneeling and says the absolution in the first person plural as a prayer for pardon (BCP 80). The confession is always optional at Morning Prayer. If the confession of sin is omitted, the officiant may still begin with an opening sentence, saying or singing it, and then move to the opening versicle.

b. Invitatory and Psalms

The cantor sings the antiphon on the invitatory psalm, and the people repeat it. The cantor then sings the verses of the psalm (*Venite, Jubilate,* or Psalm 95), pausing after each paragraph as the text is printed in *The Book of Common Prayer* (BCP 82-83) and leading the people in the antiphon. If a setting of the invitatory that does not use the antiphons is sung, the cantor leads the people in singing it. The prayer book does not expect antiphons to be used with the Easter invitatory *Pascha nostrum,* considering the repeated alleluias to be the antiphon.

If an office hymn is to follow the invitatory, it is led by the cantor. If a plainsong hymn is sung, the cantor may precent the opening line, the people joining in at the second line.

The prayer book permits the congregation to stand or sit for the psalms. Unless the psalms are very brief, it is usually best to sit. Historically, the morning psalmody concluded with the *laudes* psalms (148-150) from which the name *lauds* is derived. Howard Galley, in *The Prayer Book Office,* suggests a table of psalms of praise to be used daily at the conclusion of the psalmody (p. xxii). If this tradition is followed, it is proper to sit for the psalms and then to stand for the final psalm of praise. The psalms may be sung in any of the ways described above in section 2.C.a. The *Gloria patri* may be sung at the conclusion of each psalm, and is always used at the conclusion of the final psalm. An inclusive language alternative is provided in the *Supplementary Liturgical Materials* authorized by General Convention: "Praise to the holy and undivided Trinity, one God: as it was in the beginning, is now, and will be for ever." If it is desired to use psalter collects at the conclusion of each psalm, as suggested in An Order of Worship for the Evening (BCP 113), the officiant stands after the psalm (or after the *Gloria* and antiphon, if they are used), and with hands in the orans position says or sings, "Let us pray," and after a brief pause for silent prayer, the appointed psalter collect. Psalter collects are found at the conclusion of each psalm in the Canadian *Book of Alternative Services,* and in the Minister's Desk Edition of the *Lutheran Book of Worship.* Both books use the prayer book translation of the psalms.

c. Readings and Canticles

All sit for the readings. The reader goes to the lectern and reads the first lesson. In the announcement of the reading the short form of the titles of biblical books is preferable: "A Reading (Lesson) from First Corinthians," rather than "A Reading (Lesson) from the first letter of blessed Paul the Apostle to the Corinthians." At the end of the reading, the reader says, "The Word of the Lord," and all respond, "Thanks be to God." Silence for reflection may be kept after the reading (BCP 84). If this is done, it is important that the congregation know how long the silence will be, so that they may use the time. While this silence works well with congregations that celebrate the office together regularly, in other congregations it may simply disrupt the flow of the service. It is, of course, a monastic element, which may not be appropriate in a cathedral office.

All stand for the canticle, and, if two lessons are to be read, sit at its conclusion for the second lesson. It is customary in many places for all to make the sign of the cross at the first verse of the gospel canticles (*Benedictus, Magnificat,* and *Nunc dimittis*). The canticles should be sung in one of the modes described above for singing the psalms. A table of canticles for the various days of the week is found on page 144 of *The Book of Common Prayer.* In addition to the canticles in the prayer book, there are additional canticles and alternative translations authorized in *Supplementary Liturgical Materials,* including "A Song of Wisdom" and "A Song of Pilgrimage."

If a sermon is to be preached at Morning Prayer it may follow the final lesson. If three lessons are read this produces a pattern of reading, canticle, reading, canticle, gospel, sermon, creed, which is similar to the eucharistic Word liturgy. If only one or two lessons are read, the canticle follows the sermon. Alternatively, the sermon may be preached "at the time of the hymn or anthem after the Collects" (BCP 142).

A sermon is not normally a part of the celebration of the daily office, although there may be occasions when it is desirable. A true sermon based on the readings best follows the final reading. This is certainly to be preferred if the office is used as the Word liturgy of a celebration of the eucharist. A more general address, not closely tied to the readings, may follow the collects, either before or after the hymn or anthem. It is also permissible to preach "after the Office" (BCP 142), producing Morning Prayer and Sermon.

Non-biblical readings, such as those in J. Robert Wright's *Readings for the Daily Office from the Early Church* and *For All the Saints*, a publication of the Anglican Church of Canada, may follow the last reading, or be separated from it by a period of silence. The reader goes to the lectern, announces the reading, and reads it. At its conclusion the reader may say, "Here ends the reading," or simply stop and sit down.

A reading from the gospel may be read by a lector in the same way as the other readings, or it may be read by a deacon (or a priest, in the absence of a deacon) in the same manner as the gospel reading at the eucharist, including a gospel procession with lights and incense. The reader may cense the book at the announcement of the gospel and the congregation may make the customary responses. More simply, the deacon may read the gospel, the people standing and making the responses before and after it. Incense may be added to a standing incense burner before the reading.

d. Creed, Suffrages, and Collects

Following the final canticle, or the third reading if three are used, all stand for the Apostles' Creed. The officiant begins the creed standing in place. There is no reason for those in choir pews to turn and face the altar during the creed, although in some places this nineteenth-century custom intended to underscore the altar-centeredness of worship is well established. The creed may be omitted from one of the offices on weekdays (BCP 142), and if both Morning and Evening Prayer are celebrated daily, a uniform decision about which office will include the creed should be made in order to avoid confusing the congregation. The creed may be sung or said. Most frequently, it is monotoned if it is sung.

The people may stand or kneel for the Lord's Prayer and the following suffrages and collects (BCP 97), but the officiant remains standing. He or she faces the people (if the presider's place does not already face them) to say (or sing), "The Lord be with you," then (resuming the original position), "Let us pray," and, extending the arms in the orans position, begins the Lord's Prayer.

The officiant or a cantor sings the versicles (marked "V." in the prayer book) of either form of the suffrages, or of the third form in *Supplementary Liturgical Materials*. Suffrages A are identical with those for Evening Prayer; both Suffrages B and the supplementary form are specific to the morning. Suffrages B have been traditionally associated with the *Te Deum*, and, although it is certainly appropriate to use them when that canticle is sung, they can also be said on other occasions. Note that it is permissible for someone other than the officiant to say the versicles. This is particularly helpful if the officiant does not sing well and the suffrages are to be sung.

The collect of the day may be said at the conclusion of the suffrages. *The Book of Common Prayer* does not give any rules for the use of the various collects. It is always appropriate to use the collect for the day when there is a proper collect, such as on Sundays and major feasts; it is certainly permissible to use the collect from *Lesser Feasts and Fasts* when applicable. There is less reason to use the Sunday collects on the weekdays after Epiphany or Pentecost, since they tend to be of a more general nature.

The Book of Common Prayer assigns collects to Sundays, Fridays, and Saturdays. The four collects that follow should be used on Monday, Tuesday, Wednesday, and Thursday respectively. Following Howard Galley's recommendations in *The Prayer Book Office*, these collects should ordinarily be used on the designated days (after the collect of the day, if it is used), but they are omitted on major feasts and during Holy Week. This rule works well in practice. The prayer for mission is used following the collects unless the eucharist, or a form of general intercession, such as the great litany or one of the forms of the prayer of the people, follows (BCP 100).

These three (or two) collects may be sung to the same tones used for the collect at the eucharist. The chant is in *The Altar Book* and at S 447 and S 448 in the Accompaniment Edition Volume I of *The Hymnal 1982*.

e. Anthem, Hymn, and Intercessions

An anthem (sung by the choir) or a hymn (sung by the congregation) may follow. If a collection is to be taken up, this is the place to do it. The officiant may invite the people to contribute in appropriate words, such as a biblical verse, and may go to the altar and present the offering.

The Book of Common Prayer provides no fixed structure for the prayers that follow, but these are the common prayers of the people and are an important part of the cathedral office. The prayers may be led by the officiant, a deacon, a member of the congregation, or all may pray freely. The important thing is that the people be able to pray in common for their concerns: "Opportunity may be given for the members of the congregation to express intentions or objects of prayer and thanksgiving, either at the bidding, or in the course of the prayer; and opportunity may be given for silent prayer" (BCP 142). Forms similar to those used for the prayers of the people at the eucharist may be useful.

The officiant may conclude the prayers with the Prayer of St. Chrysostom (BCP 102) or some other suitable prayer. A deacon, the officiant, or a cantor sings (or says), "Let us bless the Lord." After the response, the officiant may say one of the concluding sentences, or the officiant and other ministers may leave. Alternatively, following the example of the Order for Evening, the officiant and congregation may exchange the peace and depart.

B. Sunday and Holy Day Celebration

There is no intrinsic difference between weekday and Sunday or holy day celebrations of the office, except that there may be a larger congregation and more opportunity to sing on Sundays. More of the options mentioned in the previous section, such as a sermon, an anthem, and a collection, may be used. If it is desired, the officiant may wear a cope and be accompanied by two servers carrying lighted torches, although this is more commonly done at evensong. The ministers and choir may enter in procession, accompanied by cross and torches and the singing of a hymn.

On Sundays and holy days the collect of the day is regularly used. If the office is the principal service of the day for those attending it, the readings from the eucharistic lectionary are used (BCP 888). If the office is not celebrated daily, but is attended on Sundays by those who also participate in the eucharist, it may be preferable to use the eucharistic lessons from one of the other years of the cycle, since the readings in the office lectionary are semi-continuous with the weekdays. If there is a choice between a longer and shorter version of the psalm, the longer version is more suitable, or the psalm from the daily office lectionary may be used. If possible, the gospel should be read with the ceremonial used at the eucharist.

The officiant may cense the altar at the *Benedictus* (The Song of Zechariah). The officiant goes to the foot of the altar. The thurifer brings the incense. The officiant places incense in the thurible and may bless it saying, "Be blessed by the One in whose honor you are to be burned." The officiant walks around the altar counter-clockwise, swinging the thurible. The cross may be censed separately with three swings. Alternatively, the officiant may stand in front of the altar and swing the thurible toward the altar while the canticle is sung. The officiant gives the thurible back to the thurifer and returns to the presider's chair (or stall). If it is desired to cense the people, the thurifer may cense the officiant, those in the choir, and the congregation.

During the Lord's Prayer, the suffrages, and the collects, the torchbearers may stand on either side of the officiant facing each other. At the beginning of the anthem (or hymn) they put away their torches and return to their places.

C. Morning Prayer as the Eucharistic Word Liturgy

Morning (or Evening) Prayer may be used as the Word liturgy at celebrations of the eucharist. There are two principal reasons why a congregation may choose to do this. They may wish to use Morning Prayer on some Sundays because it has been customarily done in that congregation, or they may wish to combine the daily office with a daily celebration of the eucharist instead of celebrating them separately. In this latter case the daily office lections may be used. On Sundays and major holy days the eucharistic readings are always used (BCP 888). On days for which eucharistic propers are provided in *Lesser Feasts and Fasts,* either these or the daily office readings may be used.

If Morning Prayer is used as the eucharistic Liturgy of the Word, it will regularly include all the readings appointed for the eucharist (two on weekdays and three on Sundays and major holy days) and a sermon. It must include the gospel reading. The officiant will ordinarily be the presiding celebrant of the eucharist and will wear eucharistic vestments. If some other person officiates, he or she may wear an alb (or cassock and surplice) and, if desired, a cope.

The ministers (and choir) may enter in procession with incense, cross, and processional torches to the accompaniment of a psalm, hymn, or anthem, as at other celebrations of the eucharist. This is especially fitting on Sundays and holy days. If the confession of sin is used it is best done at the place appointed in Morning Prayer.

The readings before the gospel are read by lay persons, who wear ordinary clothes unless they are already vested, as choristers or eucharistic ministers, for example. Canticles are sung after the first two lessons. If three lessons are read, the gospel follows the second canticle. A deacon (or assisting priest) reads the gospel with the customary eucharistic ceremonial. This may include a procession with torches and incense, the censing of the gospel book, and the kissing of the text at its conclusion. The carrying of two candles as a mark of honor to the presence of Christ in the gospel is the oldest and most significant of these ceremonies. Carrying a processional cross in the gospel procession tends to divert the focus from the gospel book. At the least, the congregation should stand and make the acclamations before and after the reading. Although it is permissible for a lay person to read the gospel as an ordinary office lesson, it is better to retain the customary gospel ceremonial, even if there is no deacon or other presbyter and the presider reads the gospel.

The sermon follows the gospel. If there are only two lessons, the second canticle follows the sermon. The Nicene Creed may be substituted for the Apostles' Creed (BCP 142). This substitution is best confined to Sundays and major holy days, but even then it may prove confusing to the congregation.

The Book of Common Prayer anticipates that the Lord's Prayer and suffrages will be omitted and the officiant will pass at once from the salutation following the creed ("The Lord be with you") to the collects. The prayer for mission is omitted (BCP 100) and a form of intercession fulfilling the requirements for the eucharistic prayers of the people follows the hymn or anthem. In practice this is quite awkward. It is much less so if the salutation leads into the prayers of the people, placing them immediately following the creed, as in eucharistic celebrations. The prayers then conclude with the collect of the day (from *The Book of Common Prayer* or *Lesser Feasts and Fasts*), and the service continues with the peace.

One of the eucharistic forms for the prayers of the people from *The Book of Common Prayer* or a similar form may be used for the intercessions, or the officiant may use a string of prayers that conform to the directions on page 383. The exchange of the peace forms the bridge to the eucharistic liturgy, which continues with the offertory.

On ordinary weekdays both the office and the eucharist may be celebrated quite simply, with little or no music, a brief homily, and less formal ceremony, as in the previous sections.

4. Celebrating Evensong

A. Daily Celebration

A few cathedrals and large parishes with resident choirs, as well as seminaries and religious houses, sing evensong daily. This is usually a semi-monastic office, without much ceremony except the entrance and exit of the choir. In other places, daily Evening Prayer is a "small group celebration" as described above for Morning Prayer, possibly with only the canticles sung. Evensong is often celebrated as an occasional service, not only at retreats and conferences but also on weekday evenings during Lent, or as a special choral event.

The collect for the following day is used at evensong on Saturday evenings and on the eves of feasts of our Lord, except for Holy Saturday. Proper lessons for the eves of principal holy days are also included in the lectionary, and the service is called the First Evensong of the feast. In this section we shall describe evensong as it can be done in an ordinary parish with modest resources. In the next section we shall describe Solemn Evensong as it can be celebrated on Saturdays, Sundays, and holy days.

If the church building is rectangular with a chancel choir, the choir and officiant may enter in procession. If the shape makes it possible, all may take their places individually and the officiant enter at the beginning of the office, perhaps accompanied by a lector carrying the Bible to be placed on the lectern. The officiant's place is the presider's chair, or an officiant's stall in choir, depending on the architectural arrangement of the church.

a. Lucernarium

The evening lamp-lighting as set forth in An Order of Worship for the Evening (BCP 109-114) is such a significant and traditional evening ceremony that it is desirable that it form a regular part of the evening office.

The church is not lighted more than is necessary for the people to assemble. A deacon (or the officiant) carries in a lighted candle or lamp and places it in a centrally located candlestick (or lamp stand), usually near the altar. The exact location of the candlestick will depend on the architecture of the church; in a small room, the candle might be placed on the altar. During Advent the candles of the Advent wreath are lighted and the Prayer for Light said by the officiant standing near the wreath. During Easter, the officiant goes to the paschal candle and says the Prayer for Light.

The officiant sings (or says) the opening greeting, "Light and peace, in Jesus Christ our Lord," or one of the seasonal alternatives (BCP 109). The short lesson is omitted, since the evensong readings will follow. The officiant sings (or says) "Let us pray" and the Prayer for Light (BCP 110-111). The altar candles are then lighted, and the other lights in the church turned on; during Easter, the altar candles are lighted from the paschal candle. *The Book of Common Prayer* notes, "During the candle-lighting, an appropriate anthem or psalm may be sung, or silence kept" (BCP 112). The *lucernaria* from *The Book of Occasional Services* (pages 10-17) are intended to be "appropriate anthems"; music is in *The Hymnal 1982* Accompaniment Edition, Volume 1, at S 305-S 320. Psalm 141:1-3, 8ab with the antiphon, "Let my prayer be set forth in your sight as incense, the lifting up of my hands as the evening sacrifice," is an appropriate psalm. *The Book of Common Prayer* (BCP 112) places the anthem after the Prayer for Light, but the structure of the *lucernaria* in *The Book of Occasional Services,* ending with a versicle and responses, suggests that the prayer should follow them.

The hymn "O gracious light" is then sung in honor of the "vesper light" now lighted. During the hymn, the candle, the altar, and the people may be censed (BCP 143). If a standing incense burner is used, the officiant places incense in the burner. If a thurible is used, the thurifer brings it to the officiant, who places incense in it and blesses it saying, "Be blessed by the One in whose honor you are to be burned." The officiant censes the candle, either standing in place or walking around the candle. The altar may also be censed, although since the candle, as the symbol of the risen Christ, and the assembled people of God are the primary foci of the offering of incense, some would omit censing the altar at a service that does not use it. If the altar is censed, the officiant walks around it counter-clockwise swinging the thurible, or stands in front of the altar and swings the thurible toward it. The cross may be censed separately with three swings: traditionally these are double swings, made by starting with the thurible against the chain, swinging it out, back to the chain and out again. Many consider this too fussy and use simple single swings. The officiant then censes the people. If it is possible to cense the people by walking down the aisles or otherwise going among them, the officiant may do this. Otherwise they are censed as is customary at the eucharist. The officiant gives the thurible back to the thurifer and returns to the presider's chair (or stall). The thurifer (or a deacon) may then cense the officiant. Alternatively, the officiant may cense only the candle, or candle and altar, and the thurifer or deacon cense those in the choir and the congregation after censing the officiant.

If the candle-lighting is not used, the office may begin with the opening sentence and confession of sin, or, omitting all before it, with "Lord, hear our prayer," as described above in Morning Prayer. The hymn "O gracious light" (*Phos hilaron*) or another hymn or evening psalm, such as Psalm 134 or 141:1-3, 8ab, follows. Incense may be burned during the hymn, and the altar and people censed.

b. The Psalms

The cantor then begins the psalms (or the antiphon on the first psalm) of evensong. The psalms may be sung in any of the ways described above. If psalter collects are used, the officiant stands at the end of each psalm (or the repetition of the antiphon, if antiphons are used) and says (or sings) "Let us pray" and, after a pause for silent prayer, the psalter collect. As indicated above, psalter collects are found at the conclusion of each psalm in the Canadian *Book of Alternative Services* or in the Minister's Desk Edition of the *Lutheran Book of Worship*.

c. The Lessons and Canticles

Frequently only one lesson is read at evensong (BCP 934), but either two or three may be used. If three lessons are read the gospel lesson follows the second canticle. The lessons are read by a reader in ordinary clothes. The reader comes to the lectern, announces the lesson, reads it, says "The Word of the Lord," and returns to his or her place. A gospel lesson may be read by a deacon (or priest) with the customary eucharistic ceremonial and responses, especially if it is the third lesson.

Silence may be kept after each reading (BCP 119). If this is done, it is important that the congregation know how long the silence will be, so that they may make use of the time.

The canticles *Magnificat* (The Song of Mary) and *Nunc dimittis* (The Song of Simeon) are the traditional evensong canticles. Metrical versions of both are in *The Hymnal 1982* (Hymns 437, 438, and 499), or they may be sung to any of the available chants. If one lesson is read, the *Magnificat* and *Nunc dimittis* may be used on alternate days following the table in *The Book of Common Prayer* (BCP 145). If Compline is also to be celebrated, the *Magnificat* is always used at evensong, and the *Nunc dimittis* at Compline. If two or three lessons are read, both canticles may be used or the gospel canticle sung after the second reading and a different canticle each day sung after the first reading, as indicated in the table. If evensong is celebrated daily the table should be followed. If it is an occasional celebration, using the traditional canticles will provide continuity.

A sermon may be preached after the final lesson, although this will seldom be done on a daily basis. A brief meditation might be given or a non-biblical reading included. If evensong is used as an extra service during Lent or Advent, for example, a sermon might well be included.

d. Creed, Suffrages, and Collects

The creed is required at one of the daily offices. If it is sung (or said) at evensong, it follows the readings and canticles (and the sermon, if one is preached). The officiant begins the opening words and the people join in. It may be monotoned or recited.

The Lord's Prayer and suffrages follow. The people may kneel at the "Let us pray" before the Lord's Prayer or remain standing. The officiant normally remains standing and faces the people (if the presider's place does not already face them) to say (or sing), "The Lord be with you," then (resuming the original position) "Let us pray," and, unless holding a book, extending the arms in the orans position, begins the Lord's Prayer.

The suffrages may be sung by the officiant or a cantor. Suffrages A are a revision of the traditional Anglican office suffrages and are common to both Morning and Evening Prayer. Suffrages B are based on a Byzantine evening litany and are proper to evensong. Either set may be used. Suffrages B, in addition to being specific to evening, permits the mention of a saint's name. The saint being celebrated or commemorated that day may be mentioned, as well as the patron saint of the parish and the blessed Virgin Mary. This is a convenient way to mention the name of a saint whose celebration would otherwise be omitted, as, for example, at Sunday evensong. The traditional order is to mention Mary first, then angels, apostles, and other saints. No saint need be mentioned, or only the saint of the day may be mentioned.

Suggestions for the use of collects are given in the description of Morning Prayer. Note that An Order of Worship for the Evening also contains suitable evening collects (BCP 113). The collect for the following day is used at evensong on the eves of Sundays and feasts of our Lord, except for Easter Even. The collects may be sung or recited by the officiant.

e. Anthem, Hymn, and Close of Office

If there is an anthem, it is traditionally sung after the prayer for mission. In place of an anthem an office hymn may be sung by the congregation. A sermon may be preached before or after the anthem, although it is better placed after the final lesson. A collection may be taken during the anthem or hymn and presented at the altar by the officiant (BCP 142).

Evensong concludes with authorized intercessions and thanksgivings, as discussed above under Morning Prayer. The bishop concludes the office with a blessing (BCP 36). An Order of Worship for the Evening includes the Aaronic blessing (BCP 114) for use by a bishop or priest, and suggests that it may be used by a deacon or lay person by substituting "us" for "you." There is no reason why this cannot also be done at Evening Prayer. The same rubric permits the use of other blessings, such as the seasonal blessings in *The Book of Occasional Services* (BOS 22-29).

The blessing may be followed by a dismissal by the deacon, if there is one present, as at the eucharist, or "Let us bless the Lord" may be used. If there has been no blessing, the officiant may conclude the office with one of the closing sentences (BCP 126).

The officiant and any other vested participants may leave in procession, or, as in An Order of Worship for the Evening, the officiant may say, "The peace of the Lord be always with you," and the congregation may exchange the peace. The officiant would then leave with as little ceremony as possible.

B. Solemn Evensong

Solemn Evensong consists of a number of festal additions to the ceremonial of evensong for use on Sundays and holy days, and on their eves (including Saturday evenings). All are optional and evensong may be celebrated on any day as described above. The officiant is normally a priest and wears an alb and cope. A deacon assistant vests in a dalmatic. Grisbrooke suggests that they wear stoles as well, although as noted above this has not been customary among Anglicans. Incense, cross, and torches may be carried in the entrance procession. A deacon may carry in the lighted candle for the *lucernarium,* and a reader may carry the Bible and place it on the lectern.

The candle-lighting, as described above, will normally be a part of Solemn Evensong. The candle (or Advent wreath during Advent) is censed during the *Phos hilaron.* The altar and congregation may then be censed, as described above, or this may be done during the *Magnificat.* The gospel may be read by a deacon with procession and incense as at the eucharist, or it may simply be treated as another reading. A sermon may be preached after the (last) lesson.

If it was not done during the *Phos hilaron,* the altar and congregation may be censed during the *Magnificat,* the officiant going to the center of the altar, there receiving the thurible, putting incense in it, blessing the incense, and censing the altar. If the people were censed during the *Phos hilaron* they should not be censed again.

During the Lord's Prayer, suffrages, and collects, the servers with torches may stand facing each other on either side of the officiant. A server may hold the book for the officiant. Note that a cantor rather than the officiant may sing the versicles of the suffrages.

After the collects, an anthem or hymn is sung. If a collection is taken it is done here. The officiant may go to the altar and present the offering. The deacon or a lay person appropriately leads the intercessions and thanksgivings. The officiant concludes them with a final prayer, such as the Prayer of St. Chrysostom (BCP 126) or one of those recommended at the conclusion of the prayers of the people in the eucharist (BCP 394-395).

The officiant may sing (or say) a final blessing, such as that given in An Order of Worship for the Evening (BCP 114) or a seasonal blessing from *The Book of Occasional Services* (BOS 22-29). The deacon (or the officiant or a cantor, if there is no deacon) dismisses the people with "Let us bless the Lord," or one of the eucharistic dismissals. If the peace is to be exchanged, the officiant says (or sings), "The peace of the Lord be always with you," and the people greet one another. The procession leaves as it entered, accompanied by instrumental music, a hymn, or in silence.

C. An Order of Worship for the Evening

This cathedral form of the evening office has been mentioned above as an appropriate substitute for Evening Prayer as a corporate sung service. The order begins with the *lucernarium* as described above. After the hymn *Phos hilaron* it may continue as Evening Prayer, as described above, or with a celebration of the eucharist, beginning with the salutation and collect (BCP 112). The *lucernarium* with its accompanying prayers, hymn, and incense is a most appropriate way to begin an evening celebration of the eucharist on midweek holy days or any other occasion. It may also be used (with the inclusion of the short lesson) with the Lord's Prayer and the grace before meals, as a solemn beginning for a parish supper.

When it is celebrated as an evening office, the *Phos hilaron* is followed by a "Selection from the Psalter" (BCP 113). This permits the choice of a suitable psalm that the assembled congregation can sing, perhaps a metrical psalm to a familiar tune. At its conclusion there may be silence and the officiant may say (or sing) a psalter collect. A Bible reading (not necessarily the passage appointed from the lectionary) is read by a lay person. This might be a reading from the proper for a lesser (or greater) feast, from the previous Sunday, or from another day in the week—but one that stands alone and does not require the congregation to hear the previous lesson or the following one.

"A sermon or homily, a passage from Christian literature, or a brief silence, may follow the Reading" (BCP 113). This rubric permits a homily or meditation on the passage, the reading of a commentary on it, or some other written or spoken reflection, whether classical or contemporary. The officiant may speak from the presider's chair or stand in the pulpit. If another person leads this response, the officiant remains seated and listens.

The *Magnificat* "or other canticle, or some other hymn of praise" follows. Clearly this is to be sung by the people, the rubric making it easy to pick something they can sing.

"A litany, or other suitable devotions, including the Lord's Prayer," follows the canticle. Suffrages B from Evening Prayer is such a suitable devotion. So are the litany forms from the prayers of the people, or others known to the participants. A deacon or lay person leads these prayers. At their conclusion, the officiant leads the congregation in the Lord's Prayer, which may be introduced by saying, "Let us pray in the words our Savior taught us."

One of the collects on page 113 of *The Book of Common Prayer* or the collect of the day or season follows the Lord's Prayer. If the officiant is a priest, the blessing may follow, after which the deacon (or the officiant or a cantor) dismisses the people. The peace may be exchanged and all depart.

This order may be celebrated with simplicity, or solemnly with cope, choir, and incense. As indicated above, its opening and closing are most suitably used with evensong.

5. Noonday Prayer and Compline

These services are by their nature informal and may frequently be celebrated in meeting rooms or similar locations. Anyone may officiate, and the congregation may stand or take whatever other posture is convenient.

When they are celebrated in a church or chapel, they should follow the model of Morning and Evening Prayer. The officiant may vest in cassock and surplice (and tippet, if ordained), or in an alb, and may sit in choir, or any other place where he or she may be seen and heard. The office may be sung. Music is found in the Appendix to *The Hymnal 1982* at S 296–S 304 for An Order of Service for Noonday and S 321–S 337 for Compline, and is published separately as *Musical Settings for Noonday and Compline*, which also includes a selection of suitable office hymns.

A. Celebrating An Order of Service for Noonday

Historically, the noonday office is one of a group of "little hours": terce, celebrated mid-morning; sext, celebrated at noon; and none, celebrated at mid-afternoon. These hours corresponded to the breaks in the Roman work day. Although An Order of Service for Noonday is set up as a single service, it can be used as a framework for the "little hours." They might be used during a retreat or quiet day, but even religious communities find it difficult to maintain the little hours in the contemporary world, and many have gone to a single noonday office.

The traditional office hymn for terce is "Now Holy Spirit, ever One" (Hymn 19, 20). The first short lesson (Romans 5:5) and collect ("Heavenly Father, send your Holy Spirit into our hearts") are the themes of terce.

"O God of truth, O Lord of might" (Hymn 21, 22) is the traditional sext office hymn, although any of the noonday hymns are suitable. The second short lesson (2 Corinthians 5:17-18) and collect ("Blessed Savior, at this hour you hung upon the cross") are suitable for sext. The third collect ("Almighty Savior, who at noonday called your servant Saint Paul") and lesson (Malachi 1:11) are obvious alternatives.

"O God, creation's secret force" (Hymn 14, 15) is the traditional hymn for none, and the fourth collect ("Lord Jesus Christ, you said to your apostles") and the short lesson from Malachi are suitable, as are the second short reading and collect referring to Christ being on the cross at this hour.

In what follows, a single mid-day office is assumed.

All stand for the opening greeting, and the office hymn (if one is sung). Suitable hymns are in the noonday section of *The Hymnal 1982*.

The psalms may be said or sung, standing or sitting, in any of the ways described for the office. Most often they will be read, antiphonally or responsively. In addition to the psalms printed, other sections of Psalm 119, Psalms 19 or 67, or a selection from Psalms 120 through 133 may be used (BCP 103). If the noonday office is said daily, Howard Galley's selections from *The Prayer Book Office* (pp. 17-54) may be followed: Sundays, 23 and 67; Sundays in Eastertide, 118; Mondays, 119:17-24; Tuesdays, 119:89-96, 105-112; Wednesdays, 121 and 122; Thursdays, 124 and 126; Fridays, 119:81-88 and 130; Fridays of Christmas and Easter, 23 and 67; Saturdays, 132; Saturdays of Lent, 119:137-144, 169-176.

The short lesson may be read by the officiant or a reader directly from the prayer book, without going to the lectern. Galley recommends 2 Corinthians 5:17-18 for use on Sundays and Wednesdays, Romans 5:5 on Mondays and Thursdays, Malachi 1:11 on Tuesdays and Saturdays, and 2 Timothy 2:11b-12a (which is not printed in the prayer book but clearly permitted by the rubric) for Fridays. The readings may be chanted. Music is in *The Hymnal 1982* Appendix (S 301–S 304), as well as in *Musical Settings for Noonday and Compline*.

The officiant stands for the Lord's Prayer and the collect. The people may stand or kneel. Only one collect is used. A reasonable practice is to use the collect of the day on Sundays and major feasts and one of the four collects provided (BCP 107) on other occasions.

B. Celebrating Compline

Compline originated in the dormitory prayers of Christian monastic communities. Because it was celebrated in the dormitory without books, it was almost unchanging in structure. This and its intrinsic appropriateness for the end of a Christian's day have made compline quite popular among contemporary Christians. It is often used to conclude evening meetings, and at retreats and conferences.

Like noonday prayer, compline may be celebrated anywhere and anyone may officiate. It is somewhat more likely to be sung, at least in part.

If it is celebrated in a church or chapel the officiant may enter at the beginning of the office, or be already in place and stand to begin the office. All make the sign of the cross at "The Lord Almighty grant us a peaceful night and a perfect end" (BCP 127). The officiant and people may kneel for the confession, although it is not required. The traditional practice of kneeling on fast days (chiefly Fridays and the weekdays of Lent) and standing on other days is probably too confusing to be practical. If the confession is said kneeling the officiant does not stand for the prayer for forgiveness at its close, nor make the sign of the cross over the congregation during it. It is appropriate for all to cross themselves during the prayer. Note that *The Book of Common Prayer* does not restrict this prayer for forgiveness to priests (BCP 128). If Compline is sung, the confession and prayer for forgiveness are said.

The psalms may be sung or said, sitting or standing. All may be used, or some selected. The first two psalms (4 and 31) and the last two (91 and 134) make convenient alternate choices.

The short lesson is read by the officiant or a reader. Everyone else sits. Any of the passages printed "or some other suitable passage" may be used (BCP 131). The reader need not go to the lectern. The readings are set to music for chanting in *The Hymnal 1982* Appendix, S 327–S 330. They are also in the pamphlet *Musical Settings for Noonday and Compline*.

Any of the hymns in the Compline section of *The Hymnal 1982*, and many of those in the evening section, are suitable as an office hymn. The hymn "To you before the close of day" (Hymn 44, 45) is most often associated with Compline, but other hymns, such as Thomas Ken's "All praise to thee, my God, this night" (Hymn 43) or the Mozarabic and Ambrosian "O Christ, you are both light and day" (Hymn 40, 41) are equally traditional. All stand for the hymn and the responsory following.

If the responsory "Into your hands, O Lord" is sung, the versicles may be sung by a cantor; both a simple and a more complex setting are given at S 331–S 333 in the Appendix to *The Hymnal 1982*. The officiant sings (or says) "Lord, have mercy," and begins the Lord's Prayer. The people stand or kneel. The officiant sings (or says) "Lord, hear our prayer," and "Let us pray," extending and opening the arms and then bringing the hands together. The officiant, with hands in the orans position, sings (or says) one of the Compline collects (BCP 133). If the officiant is holding a book, the gestures are omitted and the book held with both hands. One of the additional prayers may be added (BCP 134) and a period of silence kept. The officiant may invite the congregation to add their own intercessions and thanksgivings.

The Song of Simeon (*Nunc dimittis*) may be sung, even if the rest of the service has been said. The antiphon and canticle are sung (or said) by all standing. A metrical version of the canticle is Hymn 499 in *The Hymnal 1982*. The antiphon may be said before and after it.

All remain standing for the dismissal and blessing. The blessing is not restricted to priests, but is a prayer in the first person plural. If the sign of the cross is made, all make it on themselves.

6. Vigil of the Resurrection

The Canadian *Book of Alternative Services* contains a Vigil of the Resurrection for Saturday Evenings. This is an adaptation of an early Christian vigil looking forward to the celebration of the resurrection on the Lord's Day. Held late Saturday evening, the vigil commemorates "the myrrh-bearing women" who brought spices to the tomb before dawn on the first Easter. Like An Order of Worship for the Evening in the American prayer book, this is a form of the cathedral office. Much of the material in

The Book of Alternative Services is taken from the ecumenical office book *Praise God in Song,* which includes musical settings. This service is fittingly celebrated in the church or by a family group at home. If it is done in church, the presider may wear an alb (and cope).

The vigil begins with the Service of Light (BAS 61-65; BCP 109-112) and continues with Psalm 118:1-4, 14-29, the traditional Easter psalm, followed by a psalter collect. This is followed by Psalm 150 as an introduction to the proclamation of the resurrection gospel, which is the core of the service. One of the gospel accounts of the resurrection is then read (BAS 135). If the vigil is solemnly celebrated in church, this may be (read or) sung by a deacon with full eucharistic ceremonial.

A baptismal memorial follows. The congregation may process to the font, or gather around a bowl of water. The form in the Canadian book is similar to that in the Consecration of a Church in the American book (BAS 135-136; BCP 570).

Chapter Two

Proper Seasonal Liturgies

There are a number of proper liturgies for various occasions in the church year included in *The Book of Occasional Services*. Those which are part of the Easter Cycle are included in my previous volume, *Lent, Holy Week, Easter, and the Great Fifty Days*. The paschal mystery of the dying and rising again of Jesus Christ, however, is so central to Christian life and worship that it is difficult to say any liturgical celebration is not paschal in character. The mystery of the Christian year is one. We do not celebrate one gospel on Christmas and another on Easter. Whatever the day or season, we look into the core of the central mystery of our participation in the death and resurrection of Christ. We do this in the light of the parousia in Advent, the incarnation at Christmas and Epiphany, the atonement on Good Friday, and the ongoing mission of the church in the season after Pentecost. Yet these services are not temporally a part of the Easter cycle.

1. Lessons and Carols

This traditional English service has become quite popular in North America. Perhaps the regular broadcasting of the Christmas Eve service from King's College, Cambridge is partially responsible, as well as the fact that Christmas music is well-loved despite its commercial use in shopping malls. The secularization of so much of American society has meant that carols are no longer sung in public schools, so there many forces at work.

Two forms of this service are included in *The Book of Occasional Services:* an Advent Festival of Lessons and Music and a Christmas Festival of Lessons and Music. The Church of England publication *The Promise of His*

Glory also contains a number of carol services for Advent, Christmas, and Epiphany, including the form from King's College, Cambridge. This service was first drawn up by Edward Benson when he was Bishop of Truro for use in his cathedral, and was later adapted by Eric Milner-White for use in King's College, Cambridge, in 1918. Milner-White wrote the bidding prayer with which it is introduced.

Although the two services are parallel, we shall treat them separately.

A. Advent Festival of Lessons and Music

The church is adorned as for Advent, in violet or blue. The officiant may wear a cassock, surplice, tippet, and hood, or an alb and cope. The Advent wreath is placed where it can be lighted. There is no need for additional liturgical assistants, except to light the candles, but the choir and officiant may enter and leave in procession, preceded by cross and processional torches. If the service is in the morning, the entrance, which may be accompanied by music, will be followed at once by the bidding prayer, the Advent wreath being lighted before the service. If the service is in the evening, it begins with the Service of Light from *The Book of Common Prayer* (BCP 109ff). The Advent form of that service begins with the acclamation "Light and peace, in Jesus Christ our Lord," and the lighting of the Advent wreath while the Advent *lucernarium* or Psalm 85:7-13 is sung (BOS 31). The altar candles and the congregation's candles (if they are used) are also lighted. The officiant then says or sings the collect for Advent 1 as the Prayer for Light. The Advent hymn "Creator of the stars of night" (Hymn 60) may replace the *Phos hilaron.*

The officiant (comes to the center of the chancel and) says the bidding prayer, concluding with the Lord's Prayer and a brief blessing. Nine lessons are traditionally read, but fewer may be used. If possible, each lesson is read by a different reader. The lesson from Genesis 3 is always used. The lessons may be read with announcement and conclusion, as in the daily office, or they may be read without either (BOS 31). The final lesson may be from Luke 1, either the annunciation to Zechariah or to Mary. The gospel lesson is customarily read either by the officiant or the rector.

Music follows each reading. Advent hymns, canticles, and anthems are appropriate. Congregational hymns, choir anthems, and solos may all be used. After the final reading and hymn, the officiant says (or sings) the collect for Advent 3 or 4 and concludes the service with the Advent seasonal blessing.

This service is suitable during the Advent season. The readings look forward to the Christmas event but do not preempt its proper celebration. It is important that the music be Advent music, not Christmas carols. If the annunciation gospel is read as the final lesson, then Marian hymns, including some in the Christmas section of *The Hymnal 1982*, such as "Lo, how a Rose e'er blooming" (Hymn 81) may precede or follow it.

B. Christmas Festival of Lessons and Music

This form of the service is intended for use during the Twelve Days of Christmas. It includes an adaptation of Eric Milner-White's bidding prayer. The altar is vested for Christmas and the church decorated with greens and Christmas flowers. The officiant may wear a festal cope, or cassock, surplice, tippet, and hood. The choir and officiant may enter in procession preceded by cross and processional torches. All of the candles of the Advent wreath, including the Christ candle, are lighted. If the service is in the morning, all may enter to music, and the service begins directly with the bidding prayer. If the service is in the evening, it may begin with the Service of Light. The officiant says (or sings), "Jesus Christ is the light of the world," (BCP 109, BOS 38) and while the Christmas *lucernarium* or Psalm 113 (BOS 38) is sung the altar candles, all of the candles of the Advent wreath, and the congregation's candles (if they are used) are lighted. The officiant then says (or sings) the collect for Christmas 1 as the Prayer for Light; the *Phos hilaron* or a suitable Christmas hymn is then sung. "O Savior of our fallen race" (Hymn 85, 86), with its references to Christ as light, is suitable.

The lessons are read as in the Advent service, with appropriate Christmas music intervening. More of the appointed lessons are from the gospels. The final lesson is from the first chapter of John, although it may be omitted and the Lucan nativity story used as the final reading instead.

After the final lesson and its music, the officiant, from the chair or from the center of the chancel, says a Christmas collect and the Christmas seasonal blessing. The choir and officiant leave, usually to the accompaniment of music.

Obviously, this festival can be a choir festival in which the choir performs a number of Christmas pieces, or it can be a congregational hymn sing, in which all the familiar Christmas carols are sung. Usually it combines some of each, with the people singing several familiar Christmas hymns, and the choir performing anthems and unfamiliar or difficult songs. In many parishes it finds a place in the schedule on the Sunday after Christmas.

2. Blessing of the Creche

St. Francis of Assisi is credited with introducing the Christmas creche into the churches of the West upon his return from the Holy Land. It has become a fixture in most churches, and *The Book of Occasional Services* provides for a Station at a Christmas Creche (BOS 36-37). The text given consists of two alternative versicles and responses and collects. The material may be used in two different ways.

It may be used as a part of a procession in which all of the figures of the nativity scene are carried and put in place. This is frequently done at a children's service on Christmas Eve. The creche figures may be placed on the altar or in the sanctuary. A different child carries each figure in the procession as they go around the church to the creche, singing appropriate Christmas music. When they arrive at the creche, the presider and the deacon(s) or acolyte(s) help the children place the figures in the creche. When all are in place, the presider sings (or says) the versicle, the congregation makes the response, and the presider sings (or recites) the collect. If it is the custom of the parish, the priest may cense the creche and sprinkle it with holy water. The procession then continues to the sanctuary. This may precede a celebration of the eucharist, evensong, lessons and carols, or a Christmas pageant. The presider may wear a cope.

This station may also be made at any of the Christmas celebrations of the eucharist as a part of the opening procession. The procession is formed in the usual way, with thurifer (if incense is used), crucifer and processional torches, choir, acolytes, assisting clergy, deacon, and presider. If the presider wears a cope, the deacon and acolyte may walk on either side to hold its ends. It may start from the church door or the altar. It stops, literally "makes a station," at the creche. Before the first Christmas eucharist, the figure of the Christ child may be carried in the procession and placed in the manger by the presider. The presider sings the versicle and, after the response, the collect. The presider may cense the creche and sprinkle it with holy water. The music then resumes, or another hymn is begun, and the procession completes its course to the sanctuary for the beginning of the eucharist.

3. Service for New Year's Eve

December 31 is not only the eve of the Feast of the Holy Name, but also New Year's Eve in the civil calendar. Indeed, there is good reason to believe that the various holy days (the Solemnity of Mary, the Circumcision of Christ, the Feast of the Holy Name) observed on January 1 were intended partially at least to be a counterweight to the "pagan" festivities of the New Year. *The Book of Occasional Services* includes a service for New Year's Eve, which may either be a eucharist or a non-eucharistic service of thanksgiving and rededication. The service most appropriately leads up to the celebration of the New Year at midnight, although it can be celebrated earlier in the evening for a good reason.

If the service is a eucharist, the presider will wear eucharistic vestments. If it is not, the presider may vest in alb and stole, or alb, stole, and cope, or wear cassock and surplice.

The rite begins with the Service of Light (BCP 109), as described in the section on evensong above. The short lesson is omitted. The collect for the First Sunday after Christmas is the proper Prayer for Light (BOS 42). The Christmas *lucernarium* (BOS 12) may be used. After the *Phos hilaron* two or more lessons from among those given in *The Book of Occasional Services* are read. Each lesson is read by a lay person. Each is followed by a psalm or canticle and a psalter collect as indicated (BOS 42-45). The psalms may be sung or recited in any of the methods described for the offices. The collects are said by the presider. If several priests are present they may share the reading of the collects. The final reading is from the New Testament, although more than one New Testament reading may be used. None of the passages appointed is from the gospels. A homily may follow the readings.

If the service is held over the turning of the year, the homily should be finished before midnight so that the year may begin with "an act of self-dedication" (BOS 46), such as prayer 61 or 62 from *The Book of Common Prayer* (BCP 832-833). This prayer is said by everyone together kneeling.

The Book of Occasional Services says that the service may continue in one of three ways (BOS 46). "With the recitation of the Great Litany or some other form of intercession" retains a penitential flavor. The litany can be recited (or sung) by all kneeling, or it may be sung in procession. If it is done kneeling, the officiant, or other person leading the litany, may kneel at a litany desk in the center of the congregation, or in front of the altar in the sanctuary, or in the midst of the chancel.

If it is sung, the music is at S 67 in *The Hymnal 1982.* The Accompaniment Edition contains the entire text pointed to be sung. If it is sung in procession, the procession sets out from the altar, or from wherever the lessons were read, led by cross and torchbearers. If incense is used, the thurifer walks in front of the processional cross. The procession ideally includes the entire congregation, the presider walking last. All stand in place while the opening petitions to the Trinity are sung, and the procession begins to move around the church at "Remember not, Lord Christ, our offenses." The people join the procession as it moves through the church. The litany may be sung by a cantor walking directly behind the processional cross. The cantor may wear a cope, but ordinary choir dress is equally appropriate. If there is not enough space for the congregation to join in, then only the choir, servers, and clergy process. It may be necessary for the procession to go around the church more than once.

The procession should return to a place in front of the altar before the "Lord, have mercy." The presider then begins the Lord's Prayer standing in place. The presider or the cantor sings the versicle, "O Lord, let thy mercy be showed upon us," and, after the response, the presider sings (or says) "Let us pray" and the collect (BCP 153) and any additional prayers, concluding with the Grace (BCP 154).

If the second option is followed—"the singing of *Te Deum laudamus* or some other hymn of praise, followed by the Lord's Prayer, the Collect for Holy Name, and a blessing or dismissal, or both"—the people stand and sing together the *Te Deum* or some other suitable hymn of praise. It is traditional to ring handbells (and the tower bell) during the singing of the *Te Deum,* and this is begun at midnight to welcome the New Year. Two metrical versions of the *Te Deum* are in *The Hymnal 1982:* "O God, we praise thee, and confess" (Hymn 364) and "Holy God we praise thy Name" (Hymn 366). If it is desired, incense may be burned in the church during the singing of *Te Deum.* The *Te Deum* may be brought to a close by singing the versicles and responses from Suffrages B for Morning Prayer (BCP 98, Hymnal S 53), which are traditionally associated with it. The cantor or presider may sing the versicles.

The presider then invites the congregation to join in the Lord's Prayer, saying, "Let us pray in the words our Savior taught us." After the Lord's Prayer, the presider sings (or says) the collect for the Holy Name (BCP 213) and gives a blessing. This may be done from the presider's chair or standing in front of the altar. The Christmas seasonal blessing (BOS 23), the Aaronic blessing (BCP 114), or one of the other blessings from *The Book of Common Prayer* or *Supplementary Liturgical Materials* may be used. A deacon or cantor, or the presider, may then dismiss the people.

The third alternative begins a celebration of the eucharist with the *Gloria in excelsis* or some other hymn of praise, and begins the year with the celebration of the Feast of the Holy Name. This is a festal celebration on a principal feast of our Lord and is generally treated as a Sunday eucharist. It also appropriately begins with the New Year at midnight, but may be celebrated earlier.

4. Candlemas Procession

Candlemas is the popular name for the Feast of the Presentation of Our Lord in the Temple. It is the fortieth day after Christmas, February 2, and is the last of the Christmas cycle of feasts. In medieval England the greens that had adorned the (unheated) church since Christmas were taken down after Candlemas and replaced with box until Ash Wednesday. The Greek name for the feast is *Hypapante*, or Meeting, emphasizing the meetings between the infant Jesus and the aged Simeon and Anna. The West has generally called it the Purification of the Blessed Virgin Mary and numbered it among the Marian feasts, although it is properly a feast of our Lord. The procession began in the fifth century in Jerusalem and was always part of the Byzantine festival. It was introduced into Rome in the late seventh century, where it had a penitential character it did not entirely lose until 1970. Its origin is clearly Greek and its inspiration the Song of Simeon, with its reference to "a light to enlighten the nations." The custom of blessing candles on this day is not as old as the procession, and appeared only in the tenth century in Germany and the twelfth century in Rome.

The procession is intended to precede the eucharist on this day. A procession with candles is obviously more effective at night, and since February 2 is usually a weekday, the procession will normally precede an evening eucharist. When the Presentation occurs on Sunday it may, of course, be held before the regular Sunday eucharist. The significance of the procession is expressed in the collect said before it:

God our Father, source of all light, today you revealed to the aged Simeon your light which enlightens the nations. Fill our hearts with the light of faith, that we who bear these candles may walk in the path of goodness, and come to the Light that shines for ever, your Son Jesus Christ our Lord. (BOS 54)

The church is adorned for a festival. The color is white. The presider is vested for the eucharist, but may wear a cope for the procession. If it is possible, the congregation assembles in a place other than the church, such as the parish hall. Since the climate in many parts of North America does not lend itself to an outdoor procession in February, it may be necessary to begin the procession at the church door. In places where it is possible to move from the parish house to the church without going outdoors, that route may be followed, and in warm climates the procession can go outdoors and enter the front door of the church. The music for the chants of the Candlemas Procession are in the Appendix of *The Hymnal 1982* at S 340–S 343.

Unlighted candles are given to members of the congregation as they arrive. They gather in the hall, the narthex, or at the rear of the nave. The presider, deacon, servers, and choir join them. The service begins with the presider's greeting, "Light and peace, in Jesus Christ our Lord." During the singing of the Song of Simeon the candles are lighted. The acolyte holds the celebrant's candle. The presider sings (or says) the Prayer for Light. The procession forms:

(Thurifer)

Torch   Crucifer   Torch

Choir

Congregation

Servers

Assisting Clergy

Acolyte
Deacon(s)
Presider

The deacon says (or sings), "Let us go forth in peace," and the people respond, "In the name of Christ. Amen." The procession moves toward the church, or up the center aisle. The acolyte gives the presider a candle to carry in the procession. Appropriate hymns, psalms, or anthems are sung during the procession. A station may be made during the procession, at which the presider says or sings a collect appointed in *The Book of Occasional Services*. If the procession has begun in another place, the collect is said as the presider enters the church. If the procession has been entirely within the church, it can be said at the chancel step. As the procession moves up the center aisle, the members of the congregation go to their places. As the procession nears the altar, selected verses of Psalm 48 with a proper antiphon may be sung (Appendix S 343).

When the procession arrives in the sanctuary, the presider goes to the chair, and the eucharist begins with the *Gloria in excelsis*. After the collect of the day, all extinguish their candles.

This procession may also be held much more simply for a small congregation. The people and priest gather with unlighted candles. They exchange the opening greeting. The candles are lighted while the Song of Simeon is sung. A metrical version of the Song of Simeon is Hymn 499, "Lord God, you now have set your servant free," or a familiar chant may be used. The presider says the collect and begins the procession with "Let us go forth in peace." A crucifer leads the procession into the church, while a familiar hymn is sung. The presider may read the station collect at the chancel step and begin the eucharist with the *Gloria in excelsis*.

5. The Rogation Procession

Although the traditional Rogation Days occur during the Great Fifty Days, they are not part of the paschal celebration, but an agricultural festival which happened to occur at that time in northern Europe. Their origin is ascribed to St. Mamertius of Vienne in the fifth century, who ordered processional litanies to be sung when his diocese was threatened by volcanic eruptions. They were adopted in England in the eighth century, and were observed with outdoor processions "beating the bounds" of the parish, walking around the perimeter of the parish blessing the fields.

The Book of Common Prayer contains three sets of propers for Rogation Days, number 19 in Various Occasions (BCP 930). They are described as "for use on the traditional days or at other times." The traditional days are the Monday, Tuesday, and Wednesday before Ascension Day, but they may be celebrated at other times when it is convenient. The blessing of the fields is intended to occur before the spring planting. Many liturgical scholars think that the penitential nature of the Rogation procession is unsuitable for Eastertide.

The propers have as their themes fruitful seasons, commerce and industry, and stewardship of creation. The first is the traditional Rogation Day theme. The procession originally took place on the Rogation Days and concluded with a special celebration of the eucharist, often a "field mass" in the field being blessed. In the United States, the Sunday before the Rogation Days (the Sixth Sunday of Easter) became known as Rogation Sunday and Rural Life Sunday, and blessings of fields were held following the Sunday eucharist in rural congregations. Some suburban congregations even processed around their parking lots!

The Rogation Procession in *The Book of Occasional Services* is intended for use either before a Rogation Day eucharist or following a Sunday eucharist.

A. The Procession Before a Rogation Day Eucharist

The procession sets out from the church. The presider may wear a cope. The deacon or presider says, "Let us go forth in peace," and all respond, "In the name of Christ. Amen." The order is:

(Thurifer)

Torch   Crucifer   Torch

Choir

Congregation

Servers

(Assisting Clergy)

Acolyte   Presider   Deacon

or

Acolyte

Deacon(s)

Presider

If the presider is wearing a cope, the deacon and acolyte may walk on either side to hold its ends. If the procession is to leave the church, which is customary, it moves down the center aisle and out the door to walk through fields or grounds. If there are plowed fields to be blessed, the presider may sprinkle them with holy water as the procession passes, and a station may be made for a prayer of blessing (BOS 104). A procession may similarly be made to a fishing fleet, a park, an office building, or factory, with the propers of the eucharist to follow chosen to correspond to the occasion.

If the procession remains in the church, it follows the traditional processional route: down the center aisle to the west door, a right hand turn up the north aisle, across the front of the nave and down the side aisle, then up the center aisle to the altar. Obviously, this route assumes a rectangular church with a chancel at one end. If the church is of a different configuration, a more suitable route that takes the procession around the church is chosen.

During the procession hymns, psalms, canticles, and anthems are sung. *The Book of Occasional Services* suggests the *Benedicite* and Psalms 103 and 104, and provides proper antiphons. When the procession returns to the church the Great Litany is begun, with three additional petitions to be inserted after the petition for the bountiful fruits of the earth (BOS 104). If the procession does not leave the church, the Great Litany is sung throughout the procession. The litany concludes with the *Kyries,* at the end of which the presider begins the eucharist with "The Lord be with you," and one of the Rogation Day collects. If the Rogation eucharist is to be celebrated outdoors, the Great Litany may be sung while moving to the place where the celebration will take place, or it may be omitted. *The Book of Occasional Services* also includes additional petitions for Form V of the prayers of the people, which may be used at the Rogation eucharist if the Great Litany is not sung in procession (BOS 105).

The procession can, of course, be held three times, but most congregations will do it no more than once, unless it takes place in a farming community with the eucharist being celebrated at different farms each day.

B. The Procession Apart from the Eucharist

The Rogation Procession may also be held following the Sunday eucharist, or as a separate service in the afternoon. It makes little sense to do this unless the procession will leave the church and process to a place where fields or industry or growing things can be blessed.

If the procession follows the Sunday eucharist, it may be formed immediately after the post-communion prayer and the blessing and dismissal deferred until after the procession. If the procession follows evensong, it begins after the collects. If the procession stands alone, the servers and clergy enter to instrumental music and form the procession in the order given in the previous section. The deacon or presider says (or sings), "Let us go forth in peace" and, following the response, the procession leaves the church singing suitable psalms, hymns, or anthems. When the procession arrives at its destination the presider says the prayer of blessing from *The Book of Occasional Services* (BOS 104). The field, seed, livestock, plow, forest, factory, or fishing boat may be sprinkled with holy water. The procession may then move to another location for further blessings. After the blessing, the presider concludes the service with an appropriate prayer (several are recommended in *The Book of Occasional Services*) and blessing, and the deacon or presider dismisses the people.

6. The Baptismal Feasts

The baptismal feasts of *The Book of Common Prayer* are the Easter Vigil, Pentecost, All Saints' Day or the Sunday following, and the Baptism of Our Lord. The prayer book recommends that "as far as possible, Baptisms be reserved for these occasions or when a bishop is present" (BCP 312). If baptism is to be celebrated on these days, the ceremonies are as described in Howard Galley's *The Ceremonies of the Eucharist*. On Pentecost, the themes of resurrection and the outpouring of the Holy Spirit lead directly to the celebration of baptism following the sermon. On the Feast of the Baptism of Our Lord (the first Sunday after the Epiphany) the gospel account of Jesus' baptism provides an obvious bridge to the baptism of adults, and —with some explanation— to the baptism of infants as well. These feasts tell us we are following the example of Christ and that we too are to be anointed with the Holy Spirit and proclaimed to be the children of God by adoption and grace. All Saints' Day celebrates the communion of saints into which the baptized are born. Revelation 7:3 reminds us that we who are sealed with the cross of Christ are numbered with those who will stand in their white baptismal robes before the throne of God.

A. Baptismal Vigils

The Great Vigil of Easter (BCP 284-295) is the primary vigil celebration of the Christian church. All other vigils are derived from it. *The Book of Common Prayer* provides by rubric for a Pentecost vigil (BCP 227), which is simply a repetition of the Easter rites for a second baptismal occasion; this vigil is described in more detail in my *Lent, Holy Week, Easter, and the Great Fifty Days*. In the same vein *The Book of Occasional Services* provides baptismal vigils for the Baptism of Our Lord and for All Saints. Most congregations, unless they are baptizing adult catechumens or it is the occasion of the bishop's visitation, will wisely choose to forgo a vigil and baptize their candidate at the principal liturgy of the feast. An excellent alternative to a baptismal vigil is A Vigil on the Eve of Baptism (BOS 131-135), which looks forward to the celebration of the baptisms on the following day.

a. Vigil for the Eve of the Baptism of Our Lord

The church is adorned for the feast. The best altar hangings and vestments are used; usually these are white, gold, or silver. The presider wears a chasuble or cope and the deacon a dalmatic.

The vigil begins with the Service of Light (*lucernarium*) as described in chapter one. The Epiphany *lucernarium* (BOS 13) may be used. The collect for the First Sunday after Christmas is the proper Prayer for Light (BCP 213). The *Gloria in excelsis* may replace the *Phos hilaron* (BOS 51), although it is reasonable to use the latter since it is an evening celebration. The collect for the Baptism of Our Lord follows the *Gloria* or *Phos*, and three or more of the lessons in *The Book of Occasional Services* are read before the gospel, each followed by a period of silence and a psalm (BOS 51). Canticles or hymns may also be used. Psalter collects may follow the psalms, as at the Easter Vigil. The proper readings and psalm for the feast should be included, although *The Book of Occasional Services* does not require this and offers Matthew 28:1-10, 16-20 as an alternative gospel.

Baptism (or confirmation, if that is the occasion for the vigil) follows the gospel and sermon, as at the Sunday eucharist. *The Book of Occasional Services* permits the Renewal of Baptismal Vows, although it is difficult to imagine why a non-baptismal vigil would be scheduled.

After the baptism and chrismation, the eucharist continues. Newly baptized adults and godparents of baptized children bring up the gifts at the offertory (BCP 313). The Epiphany seasonal blessing (BOS 24) followed by dismissal by the deacon forms an appropriate conclusion to the liturgy.

b. Vigil for the Eve of All Saints' Day
The baptismal vigil for All Saints' Day or the Sunday after All Saints' Day is, except for the propers, identical to that described in the previous section. The All Saints' *lucernarium* (BOS 15), the Festivals of Saints Prayer for Light (BCP 111), the collect for All Saints' Day, and the All Saints' seasonal blessing (BOS 28) are used.

c. Vigil on the Eve of Baptism
This service (BOS 131-135) is very different from the two that precede it, since it looks forward to the baptism being celebrated on the following day. When it takes place on the eve of a baptismal feast, the proper collects, psalms, and readings for those vigils are used. On other occasions, psalms and readings from those listed for this service (BOS 131), and any appropriate collect, are chosen. The collect At Baptism (BCP 254) is the obvious choice, unless the collect of the day is especially apt.

The church is decorated for the following day, and the altar hangings and vestments are of that day's color. The presider may wear an alb, stole, and cope and the deacon an alb, stole, and dalmatic, or both may wear alb and stole. The vigil begins with the Service of Light (BCP 109). After the *Phos hilaron,* the presider sings (or says), "The Lord be with you," and the chosen collect.

The presider sits and three or more readings follow, "each followed by a period of silence and a Psalm, Canticle, or hymn" (BOS 131). The lessons are read by lay persons. The psalms may be recited or be sung in any of the ways described above for the office. The gospel is read as at the eucharist, by a deacon (if there is one) with the customary ceremonial.

After the gospel and homily, the presider invites the candidates and their sponsors to come forward. The candidates kneel or bow their heads, and the sponsors each place a hand on the shoulder of their candidate. The presider then lays a hand on the head of each candidate in silence and leads one of two forms of prayer given in *The Book of Occasional Services* (BOS 132-135). A hymn is sung, and the presiding priest concludes the vigil with a solemn blessing, either one of the threefold seasonal blessings given in *The Book of Occasional Services,* or the Aaronic blessing from an Order of Worship for the Evening (BCP 114). The deacon (or the presider, if there is no deacon) dismisses the people.

B. The Renewal of Baptismal Vows

The Book of Common Prayer provides by rubric that if there are no candidates for baptism on the baptismal feasts, the Renewal of Baptismal Vows (BCP 292) may take the place of the Nicene Creed at the eucharist (BCP 312).

If there are no baptisms, the presider goes to the front of the altar or the chancel steps and stands facing the people. The presider then invites the people to renew the baptismal covenant, using words similar to those used for the Easter Vigil (BCP 292) but adapted to the particular occasion, and then continues with the Renewal of Baptismal Vows. The invitation may also be inserted into the baptismal rite immediately before "Let us join with *those* who *are* committing *themselves* to Christ and renew our own baptismal covenant" (BCP 303).

Michael W. Merriman has written a set of these invitations to renewal adapted to particular feasts:

Pentecost
Dear People of God: Our Lord Jesus Christ sealed the paschal mystery of his death and Resurrection in his ascension and gift of the Holy Spirit on the Day of Pentecost. That same Spirit continues to give birth to God's people by the waters of Baptism. I call upon you, therefore, (to join with those who are now to receive the Holy Spirit in Baptism, and) to renew your own baptismal covenant.

All Saints (on the day or the Sunday following)
Dear People of God: In Holy Baptism we have become part of that great fellowship of believers in all times and places: the Communion of Saints. In baptism God has adopted us as children and made us members of Christ's body and inheritors of God's kingdom with the saints in light. (Joining with those who are committing themselves to Christ) let us now renew the vows of our baptism by which God has made us a holy people.

The First Sunday after the Epiphany
Dear People of God: In Holy Baptism we follow the pattern of our Lord Jesus Christ. As he came up from the water he was anointed by the Spirit of God and designated as God's Son. So we also are anointed by that same Spirit; we are reborn and adopted as sons and daughters with whom God is well pleased. Let us now (join with those who are committing themselves to Christ and) renew our own baptismal covenant.[1]

Following the Renewal of Baptismal Vows the presider may sprinkle the people with baptismal water. A server holds a vat containing the water and the priest, using an evergreen branch or some other sprinkler, sprinkles the people.

If a fuller ceremony is desired, the priest may go in procession to the font with incense (if it is used), crucifer, and torches, fill it with water, and bless it, as at baptisms, and then invite the people to renew the baptismal covenant, sprinkling them with the newly blessed water at the conclusion of the renewal. If the procession back from the font passes through the congregation, the sprinkling may be done then. Appropriate hymns, psalms, or anthems may be sung during the procession to and from the font.

---

1. *OPEN* (Spring 1991), 11. To my knowledge these have not been published elsewhere, but were regularly used when Merriman was precentor of Grace Cathedral, San Francisco. They are included here with his permission.

Chapter Three

Pastoral Offices

The pastoral offices are rites for particular occasions in the lives of individual Christians. Unlike the eucharist, the daily offices, and Christian initiation, which are integrated into the celebration of the liturgical year, the pastoral offices are geared to the pattern of individual lives. They appear in *The Book of Common Prayer* in roughly the order in which individuals experience them. Additional pastoral services are included in *The Book of Occasional Services*.

1. Rites Related to Christian Initiation

Baptism is not among the pastoral offices of *The Book of Common Prayer*, but takes its place with the eucharist as a central sacramental rite. Since it is normally celebrated at the chief Sunday eucharist (BCP 298), it is discussed by Howard Galley in *The Ceremonies of the Eucharist*. Most of the catechumenal rites are described in my *Lent, Holy Week, Easter, and the Great Fifty Days,* as is baptism in the context of the Great Vigil. If the catechumenate is to lead up to a baptism on the Feast of the Baptism of Our Lord, the Enrollment of Candidates takes place on the First Sunday of Advent and the scrutinies on the Second, Third, and Fourth Sundays (BOS 122).

A. Emergency Baptism

While emergency baptism (BCP 313-314) can certainly be described as a pastoral rite, little ceremonial direction needs to be given. Any baptized person may administer emergency baptism using the person's name (if known) and pouring water on his or her head with the words, "I baptize you in the Name of the Father, and of the Son, and of the Holy Spirit." Any available water may be used. The prayer book recommends saying the Lord's Prayer after the baptism and adding the prayer printed on page 314, but this is clearly optional, and a copy of *The Book of Common Prayer* may not be available. The person doing the baptizing should then inform the parish priest so that the baptism can be recorded in the parish register.

B. Admission of Catechumens

Unlike the enrollment of candidates, which is tied to the church year, catechumens may be admitted at any time of year (BOS 117). The section of *The Book of Occasional Services* called Concerning the Catechumenate (BOS 114-116) explains the catechumenal process and the place of this rite in it. The admission takes place within a principal Sunday liturgy. The bishop, the rector, or the priest-in-charge, presides (BOS 116).

After the sermon, the presider invites those to be admitted and their sponsors to come forward. If candidates stand on the liturgical south facing the presider and liturgical assistants on the liturgical north, it will present better visual lines for the congregation than if they stand facing east and west with their backs toward the congregation. In some buildings other arrangements may work better, such as the presider standing facing the altar with the candidates facing the congregation. The sponsors stand behind those whom they are sponsoring.

The presider asks those to be admitted, "What do you seek?" They respond, "Life in Christ." Unless the number of new catechumens is very large, each one is asked and answers individually. If any catechumen "after consultation with the celebrant, wishes to renounce a former way of worship," that occurs now. This will seldom happen in North America, but may be important if the former "way of worship" involved evil practices. The presider addresses the remaining questions to all those becoming catechumens, and the final question to the sponsors (BOS 118).

Those being admitted kneel. The sponsors remain standing and place a hand on the shoulder of the one they are sponsoring. The presider says the prayer "May Almighty God, our heavenly Father, who has put the desire into your hearts" with hands extended toward them. A server holds the book for the presider.

The sponsor presents each person being admitted as catechumen to the presider, reciting his or her name. The presider marks with the thumb a cross on the forehead of each, saying, "*N.*, receive the sign of the Cross on your forehead and in your heart, in the Name of the Father, and of the Son, and of the Holy Spirit" (BOS 118). Everyone says, "Amen," and the sponsors also mark a cross of the foreheads of their catechumens. All return to their places, and the liturgy continues.

During the prayers of the people, the new catechumens are prayed for by name (BOS 119). No further alterations in the eucharistic liturgy are made.

C. Welcoming Returning Members and Members Baptized in Other Traditions

This is the first rite in a series called Preparation of Baptized Persons for Reaffirmation of the Baptismal Covenant (BOS 139). The two following rites, Enrollment for Lenten Preparation (BOS 141-143) and Maundy Thursday Rite of Preparation for the Paschal Holy Days (BOS 144-145) are described in *Lent, Holy Week, Easter, and the Great Fifty Days*. They are preceded in *The Book of Occasional Services* by a section entitled Concerning Reaffirmation of Baptismal Vows, which describes the series of rites and stages as "a process similar to that of the catechumenate to prepare mature baptized persons to reaffirm their baptismal covenant and receive the laying on of hands by the bishop" (BOS 136). This includes those returning to active church life after a period of inactivity and those entering the Episcopal Church from another tradition (BOS 138). The process may also be used for penitents, "persons who have been separated from the Church due to notorious sins" (BOS 136).

This rite is designed to make the passage from the stage of inquiry to one of formation and deeper exploration of faith and ministry. It takes place at the principal Sunday eucharist. Those being welcomed are prayed for by name during the prayers of the people. After the prayers, the senior warden or other representative of the community presents them to the presider (BOS 139). The suggestions about placement of the participants made in the previous section applies here also. It is better if all are placed so that those being welcomed do not have their backs to the people.

The initial question, "What do you seek?" is asked of each person individually. The remaining questions are addressed to the group, except for the last two, addressed to the sponsors and to the congregation respectively. The sponsors place a hand on the shoulders of those being welcomed and the presider prays over them with extended hands (BOS 141). A server hold the book for the presider.

The baptized persons being welcomed then sign their names in the church's register of baptized members. The book may be placed on the altar for them to sign, or on a table or stand located closer to the people if that is more convenient. A deacon stands beside the book to assist in the signing and reads the names aloud as they are written. If there is no deacon, some other person stands beside the book, and the sponsor speaks the name aloud as it is written.

When all have signed, the presider says, "Please welcome the new members of the community." All respond: "We recognize you as members of the household of God. Confess the faith of Christ crucified, proclaim his resurrection, and share with us in his eternal priesthood" (BOS 141). As in the baptismal rite, where a similar invitation usually produces applause rather than a verbal response, it may be necessary to wait for applause to die down before the deacon and servers lead the response.

The service continues with the peace, at which the new members and the faithful exchange greetings. Some of those being welcomed may read the lessons, present the bread and wine, or fulfill other liturgical functions appropriate to lay members of the congregation.

D. Confirmation, Reception, and Reaffirmation

Confirmation, according to the Catechism, "is the rite in which we express a mature commitment to Christ, and receive strength from the Holy Spirit through prayer and the laying on of hands by a bishop" (BCP 860). There is no theological discussion of reception and reaffirmation in *The Book of Common Prayer*, but separate formulas are provided for them. As Howard Galley remarks, "Since the laying on of hands has historically been associated with blessings of all kinds, it is recommended for use at reception and reaffirmation as well."[1]

---

1. Galley, *Ceremonies of the Eucharist*, 221.

There is no consensus at the present time as to which baptized adults coming into the Episcopal Church should be confirmed and which received. Daniel Stevick, in the best contemporary discussion of this question, concludes:

> No distinction should be made between baptized Christians of mature faith who come to the Episcopal Church from other communions. Such persons are all fully initiate sacramentally, and they are all at this occasion doing the same thing, viz., promising to carry out the obligations of their baptism in the responsibilities and satisfactions of the Episcopal community of faith. If the distinction between receiving Catholics and confirming Protestants is not required as a matter of principle, in our ecumenical era it should be a matter of principle to see that it is discontinued.[2]

It is recommended, following Stevick's conclusion, that all baptized adults entering the Episcopal Church be received by the bishop with the laying on of hands, and as Galley recommends, that those reaffirming their baptismal vows be similarly received. In other words, the ceremonial in all three cases will be the same, with the appropriate form of words used.

In *The Book of Common Prayer* confirmation is included within the rite of baptism, since it is assumed that it will be most frequently administered when the bishop visits a parish to preside at the parish eucharist and baptize. Confirmation is also included among the pastoral offices for the convenience of the congregation on those occasions when there are no baptisms. *The Ceremonies of the Eucharist* gives detailed directions for both possibilities in the section on The Bishop at Holy Baptism.

It should be noted that the ceremonial Galley recommends is different from that prescribed in the Roman Catholic rite, in which the bishop, using a declarative formula, anoints the confirmands while seated and wearing

---

2. Daniel B. Stevick, "To Confirm or To Receive?" in *Baptism and Ministry*, Liturgical Studies 1, ed. Ruth A. Meyers (New York: Church Hymnal Corporation, 1994), 78-79. For further discussion of the theological issues surrounding these rites see also Charles P. Price's "Rites of Initiation" in the same volume, pages 86-102, and Leonel L. Mitchell, "What Shall We Do about Confirmation?" in *A Prayer Book for the 21st Century*, Liturgical Studies 3, ed. Ruth A. Meyers (New York: Church Hymnal Corporation, 1996), 104-109.

the mitre. This is the ceremonial Galley recommends when the bishop administers the baptismal chrismation. In Anglican usage, which, he reminds us, "is based on an equally venerable ancient practice," the outward sign of confirmation is the laying on of hands with prayer, for which "the traditional posture is standing with head uncovered."[3] Following Galley's recommendations is an excellent way of celebrating the 1979 initiation rites.

E. The Preparation of Parents and Godparents for the Baptism of Infants and Young Children

According to *The Book of Occasional Services,* "this process is designed to deepen the Christian formation of those who will present infants and young children for baptism" (BOS 159). It is divided into stages, each concluding with a rite. The process is parallel to the catechumenate for adults. Its use is optional.

a. The Blessing of Parents at the Beginning of the Pregnancy

The first stage is brief. In it the parents and pastor choose the godparents and schedule meetings throughout the pregnancy. It concludes with the Blessing of Parents at the Beginning of the Pregnancy. The rite is that of the Blessing of a Pregnant Woman (BOS 157-158) with a few changes to include the father. If the father is not a participant in the rite, the form for a woman is used. The changes described on pages 159 and 160 of *The Book of Occasional Services* basically involve including the father in the opening prayer.

The rite takes place at the Sunday eucharist after the prayers of the people and before the peace (BOS 160). The parents come forward, along with the godparents, and stand before the presider, who faces them and the people. The rite consists of a collect and four petitions (BOS 157). A fifth petition includes the godparents and speaks of preparation for baptism. The presider may sprinkle the parents with holy water. All join in the exchange of the peace.

---

3.   Galley, *Ceremonies,* 221.

b. Thanksgiving for the Birth or Adoption of a Child

During the second stage "the parents, their other children, and the godparents meet regularly with one or more catechists to deepen their formation in salvation history, prayer, worship, and social ministry" (BOS 160). If a parent is a catechumen, the process takes place within the catechumenate. The stage concludes with the Thanksgiving for the Birth or Adoption of a Child from *The Book of Common Prayer* (BCP 439-445).

The rite takes place at the Sunday eucharist following the prayers of the people. Prayers from the rite may also be used in the hospital or home (BCP 439). After the prayers of the people the presider invites the family "to present themselves before the Altar." The presider makes the appropriate address to the congregation (BCP 440).

If the rite is used for an adoption, the address is followed by questions to the parents, and to the child, if old enough to answer. The presider then gives the child to the parents, saying: "As God has made us his children by adoption and grace, may you receive N. as your own son (daughter)" (BCP 441). If the child is an infant, the presider takes the child and places it in the arms of the mother or father. If the child is older, the presider takes the child by the hand and places the hand in that of a parent. If there is more than one child, this is done for each. The parents then say the prayer, "May God, the Father of all, bless our child." If more than one child has been adopted, all of their names are used.

The Act of Thanksgiving follows, introduced by the presider, "Since it has pleased God to bestow...." This is done whether the child has been born or adopted into the family. The Song of Mary (*Magnificat*), Psalm 116, or Psalm 23 is then said by all. If it is sung, it should be to a simple tune so that the parents may join in.

The presider, facing the people and the family, says one or more of the concluding prayers. In the context of preparation for baptism, the prayer "For a child not yet baptized" is appropriate. The presider signs the child with the cross and announces the date of the baptism. The child is prayed for in the prayers of the people by name until the baptismal day (BOS 160). The presider blesses the family (BCP 445), and all exchange the peace.

c. Holy Baptism

The third stage normally concludes with holy baptism. *The Book of Occasional Services* expects this to take place on a major baptismal day. It includes the statement: "The infant...may receive Holy Communion (in the form of a few drops of wine if the child is not yet weaned)" (BOS 161). This is an important statement, recognizing that a baptized infant is a fully initiated member of the church and eligible to receive communion. It also suggests the best manner of communicating infants.

The baptismal rite, as mentioned above, is described by Howard Galley in *Ceremonies of the Eucharist.*

d. Adaptation for Special Circumstances

The Book of Occasional Services lists alternatives (BOS 162), such as deferring the baptism until the child is old enough to go through the catechumenate. In this case the admission to the catechumenate replaces the baptism as the final rite of stage three.

If the parents do not begin the preparation during pregnancy, then the first two stages are combined and the first rite dropped. The second may be the thanksgiving for birth or adoption, or the enrollment of the child as a candidate for baptism, suitably adapted.

If the child has received emergency baptism, the process may continue if the child survives. The baptism is recognized on the baptismal feast, with the full participation of the godparents, the child taking part in everything except the administration of the water, and being signed (and anointed) and communicated (BCP 314, BOS 162).

If the thanksgiving rite is used for the adoption of unbaptized children, it may be integrated into this process. If the children are already baptized then that prayer is used in the rite and the children receive communion at the eucharist. It is also possible to use the rite of thanksgiving for an adoption on the occasion of the baptism of an adopted child.

2. Marriage Rites

"Christian Marriage," according to its opening rubric, "is a solemn and public covenant between a man and a woman in the presence of God" (BCP 422). Marriage itself is not necessarily a Christian rite, and is described as "established by God in creation" (BCP 423) as a part of the natural order. The Episcopal Church recognizes as real marriages those contracted without any Christian rites and provides the Blessing of a Civil Marriage

(BCP 433-434) for those who wish to add the distinctive Christian rites to a marriage already contracted.

The prayers of the people of God, participation in the eucharist, and the nuptial blessing are the distinctive Christian rites connected with marriage. A priest or bishop normally presides "because such ministers alone have the function of pronouncing the nuptial blessing, and of celebrating the Holy Eucharist" (BCP 422). A deacon may "perform marriages" where it is permitted by civil law, and no priest or bishop is available. Deacons may lead the prayers of the people of God for the couple and fulfill the legal requirements, but since they cannot preside at the eucharist or pronounce the nuptial blessing, it is highly undesirable.

Both the canons of the church and the requirements of civil law regulate marriage. In the United States the Christian minister acts also as the agent of the state in witnessing the marriage. This is not the case in many other countries, where separate civil and religious ceremonies are conducted.

Marriage is also a major cultural celebration, and people come to the church's liturgy with a multitude of expectations that are sometimes at variance with the church's theology of marriage. They often have ceremonial ideas derived from bridal books or books of etiquette. Many of the customs surrounding weddings are part of particular cultures and those that are not contrary to the theological principles of the rites may be included. There are also many options in the marriage service itself. It is important that the priest and the couple agree about what is to happen well before the rehearsal.

The wedding itself may be extremely simple. Other than the presiding minister, the only necessary participants are the couple and two witnesses. Usually there is at least organ music. There may be a full choir and a sung liturgy with the same ceremonial as the Sunday parish eucharist, with bridesmaids and ushers, a ring-bearer, and flower-girls. Clergy of other churches may assist in the service, with the bishop's permission.

The marriage service has the structure of the eucharistic liturgy of the Word, and it may form a single service with the celebration of the eucharist. The celebration of the eucharist and reception of communion by the bride and groom and their guests is most fitting when they are church people, but it may be inappropriate if they are not regular communicants.

It is helpful if the parish has a set of formally adopted policies concerning weddings that are published and can be given to the couple. These should include rules about such things as flowers, decorations, music, photography, and any cost for sextons, organist, and use of facilities.

A. The Celebration and Blessing of a Marriage

According to Title I, Canon 18, the Episcopal Church normally requires thirty days' notice before a wedding. The couple must be instructed "as to the nature, meaning, and purpose of Holy Matrimony," including instruction in the theology of the rite. A rehearsal is not only a practical necessity, but also an occasion to explain to the entire wedding party the meaning of what we do and say. The rehearsal is also an appropriate time for the signing by the couple and the witnesses of the canonical declaration of intention. Many clergy find it convenient to have the parties sign the parish register and the license required by the state at this time rather than after the wedding. The officiating minister can then sign the forms after the wedding, returning the required documents to the state, and giving the appropriate certificates to the newly married couple.

Unless the wedding is to be held at the parish Sunday eucharist, the color for weddings is white. If the eucharist is to celebrated, eucharistic vestments are usually worn. If there is no eucharist, the presider may wear surplice and stole, or alb, stole, and cope.

Seating at the front of the nave is needed for the bride and groom and their attendants during the readings and homily. Chairs (or benches) placed in front of the first row of pews are often the most convenient. It may also be desirable for the bride and groom to have a place to sit near the altar while people in the congregation are receiving communion.

The readings before the gospel are read by lay persons (BCP 422). Normally the couple will choose the readers in consultation with the priest. The gospel is read by the deacon, or, if there is no deacon, by another minister or the presider.

An assisting priest or a deacon may deliver the charge, ask for the declaration of consent, deliver a homily, and lead the prayers for the couple (BCP 422). These are reasonable things to ask an assisting minister of another church to do.

If a bishop participates, the bishop should preside at the eucharist and pronounce the nuptial blessing (BCP 422).

One or two rings may be used as the couple chooses, though "when desired, some other suitable symbol of the vows may be used" (BCP 437). This permits people in other cultural traditions to follow their own customs.

If the parish tradition is for the rings and the bride and groom to be sprinkled with holy water at the blessings, then a vat filled with holy water and a sprinkler (which may be a branch) will be needed. The eucharistic elements are placed on a table from which the bride and groom may take them at the offertory.

a. Entrance Procession

The opening rubrics of the Celebration and Blessing of a Marriage pass over what is often the most difficult part of the wedding: assembling the participants and arranging their entrance into the church. Unless the wedding is extremely simple, it is impossible to proceed without a rehearsal.

There is no ecclesiastically prescribed order for a wedding procession, save that at its conclusion the woman is to be on the right and the man on the left of the presider. The priest will do well to follow any reasonable local custom.

Alternatives to the customary procedure include the bride and groom being seated with their parents rather than making a formal entrance and then coming forward at the conclusion of an opening hymn, and the bride and groom (usually together) entering with the ministers to underscore their roles as ministers of the marriage. If this second alternative is followed all may enter in a formal procession, led by thurifer (if customary), crucifer, and torchbearers, followed by choir, acolytes, ushers, bridesmaids, bride and groom, assisting clergy, and presider. A congregational hymn, a choir anthem, or organ music may accompany this procession.

More commonly, the guests and family being seated and the runner (if one is used) unrolled, the bridal procession will enter to organ music. The clergy and choir may enter in a traditional procession with cross and candles immediately before the wedding party, or they may enter simply while the bridal procession is coming down the aisle. There are many possible orders for the procession.

The groom and best man (if they are not a part of the entrance procession) enter from the transept or sacristy and stand at the front of the nave to the left of the priest, facing the people.

The ushers (walking two by two if there are many) lead the bridal procession followed by the bridesmaids, flower girls, ring-bearer, maid (or matron) of honor, and the bride, walking on her father's (or other escort's) right arm. If the bride is not to be "given away," the escort may go directly to a place in the congregation. If she prefers, the bride may simply walk alone.

However it has been accomplished, the bridal party stands facing the altar, the woman at the left of the man. If the bride is to be presented or "given away" by her father, he stands slightly behind her and may be joined by her mother. If both the bride and groom are to be presented, the groom's parents may stand behind him. The presider and any other officiating clergy stand facing them. In many churches the chancel step is a convenient location; in others it may be at the center of the communion rail, or a comparable location.

b. The Declaration of Consent

The presider, or another minister, reads the exhortation (BCP 423) facing the bride and groom. The full names of the couple are inserted at *N.N.* and *N.N.* The minister pauses slightly after "Speak now; or else for ever hold your peace" and then addresses the charge to the couple, again pausing slightly at its conclusion.

The man and woman face each other. The presider speaks directly to them. The Christian names that the couple wish to use, not necessarily their first names, are used in place of the single *N.* in the questions. The couple look at each other and respond, "I will." The presider then asks the congregation, "Will all of you witnessing these promises do all in your power to uphold these two persons in their marriage?"

If there is to be a presentation, or giving in marriage, it takes place now (BCP 437). If the presenters are not in place, they may come forward. The presider asks the question in one of the forms on page 437 of the prayer book. "I do" is the response to the presider's question. If more than one person responds, all do so together. They return to their places immediately following.

The "giving away" of the bride is not part of the main service in *The Book of Common Prayer*, but is a supplementary rite. It may either be completely omitted, or both parents may present both the bride and groom to each other. If the bride is to be "given away," the father places her hand in the priest's hand, and the priest places it in the groom's hand. Before doing this, the father may turn back the bride's veil and kiss her. Some couples will consider this medieval nonsense expressive of the view that women are property now being transferred from father to husband. Others will find a new rationale for a beloved ceremony and wish to continue it. The most worthwhile symbolic act in this is the joining of the couple's hands by the priest, which can be done whether or not there is any presentation.

"A hymn, psalm, or anthem may follow" (BCP 425). During this, the wedding party may go to the places provided for them to sit during the readings. The chairs for the bride and groom may be moved into the center of the aisle by ushers or acolytes.

c. The Ministry of the Word

The presider, standing either at the chair or in front of the altar where the declaration of consent took place, says (or sings), "The Lord be with you" and the collect. If the wedding party have not moved to their seats, they do so at the conclusion of the collect. All sit for the readings.

Normally two lessons, with a responsorial psalm between them, and the gospel are read. An Alleluia verse (except in Lent) may follow the second lesson. If only one lesson is used, the psalm follows it. The lessons are read by lay persons. They may be members of the wedding party or come from the congregation to read. The psalm may be sung in any of the ways customary at the Sunday eucharist or else recited. A hymn or anthem may replace the psalm or verse, or both. A deacon or other assisting minister reads the gospel. The ceremonial customary at the Sunday eucharist is appropriate. If there is no other ordained person participating, the presider reads the gospel.

A homily may follow.

d. The Marriage

The clergy and the wedding party return to their places. If there is a long chancel they may move to the communion rail or the foot of the altar steps, so that the bride and groom may stand facing each other before the altar. The arrangement of the church will determine where this should be. In most sanctuaries only the maid (or matron) of honor and the best man accompany the couple at this point, other attendants remaining by their seats. The traditional place for the presider is facing the couple and the congregation. Some would move the presider to the side, but close enough to be able to preside, to emphasize the role of the man and woman as the ministers of the sacrament.

The man and woman repeat their vows facing each other. Some couples wish to learn the vows and say them from memory, others wish the presider to hold the book so that they may read them, but most wish to repeat them after the presider a few words at a time. If the couple choose to say the vows from memory, the presider should be ready with a book either to prompt them, or to point to the text for them to read.

The man takes the woman's right hand in his while he makes his vow. They loose their hands, and she takes his right hand in hers to repeat her vow.

The rings are given to the presider by the bride and groom. It is easiest to have them place the rings on the open book instead of trying to pass them from hand to hand. The priest may bless the rings simply standing in place, or take them to the altar. The priest makes the sign of the cross over the rings and may sprinkle them with holy water, being careful not to damage the book. A server brings the vat of holy water to the presider.

Either person may give the ring first. The giver takes the ring from the presider and places it on the ring finger of the other's hand (BCP 427). It is often easiest to leave the ring on the book and have the giver pick it up. The presider can then hold the book under the hands to catch the ring if it is dropped. The presider helps the giver to say the words, "*N.*, I give you this ring...." The prayer book provides a non-trinitarian alternative form for use when one of the parties cannot, for reasons of conscience, invoke the Trinity, as in an inter-faith marriage.

The presider then joins the couple's right hands. If the clergy have not stood in the center facing the couple, they now move to that position. The presider traditionally wraps the stole around the couple's hands, "tying the knot," placing his or her hand on top of theirs while declaring that they are husband and wife. Some argue that the use of the stole should be avoided, since it suggests that the priest, not the couple, is the minister of marriage.

If the eucharist is not being celebrated, the presider introduces the Lord's Prayer (BCP 428). A deacon "or other person appointed" leads the prayers for the newly married couple (BCP 429). The person appointed may be another ordained minister assisting at the wedding. If no other ministers are participating in the service, the couple may wish the presider to lead the prayers, or to ask a lay person to do so.

The leader of the prayers stands in front of the couple, or at the lectern or pulpit, as convenient. It is helpful if some in the wedding party are prompted to respond loudly so that others in the congregation are encouraged to say *Amen* after each petition.

e. The Blessing of the Marriage

The bride and groom kneel at the center of the altar rail or at a prie-dieu placed for them. The presider (or the bishop) says one of the two appointed prayers with hands extended over the couple, or placed upon their heads. A server or the deacon may hold the book. If the bishop pronounces the blessing, the mitre and staff are brought. The sign of the cross is made over the couple at "bless, preserve, and keep you." If it is the custom, the presider may sprinkle the bride and groom with holy water.

The presider (or an assistant) helps the couple to stand up after the blessing. The presider introduces the peace, saying, "The peace of the Lord be always with you." The bride and groom greet each other with the kiss of peace (BCP 431). The traditional kiss of bride and groom is the only remnant of the exchange of the peace that survived the Middle Ages and the Reformation, and it is here restored to its proper context.

The newly married couple then exchange the peace with the wedding party and the presider, their family, and friends. The clergy exchange the peace with the wedding party and those in the sanctuary. It is useful to discuss beforehand how extensively the peace will be exchanged at the wedding. Some couples wish only a formal exchange with attendants and parents, while others prefer an exuberant exchange of greetings throughout the congregation.

If the eucharist is not celebrated, the service is over and the couple may desire to exchange the peace only with each other and then go to the back of the church to greet their families and friends. In this case the exit follows immediately, as soon as the bride and groom are in place to depart.

f. The Nuptial Eucharist

If the eucharist is celebrated, the presider says the offertory sentence after the greetings have subsided. The bride and groom bring the bread and wine to the altar at the offertory. If they have moved throughout the congregation exchanging greetings, the elements may be placed at a table at the back of the nave. The couple take them in their hands and bring them directly to the altar following the offertory sentence. If the couple are not exchanging greetings throughout the congregation at the peace, the elements may be placed on a table near the front of the nave, where they may get them after greeting their families.

A deacon (or assisting priest) goes to the altar to receive the elements from the bride and groom and to prepare the table. If there is no deacon or assisting priest, the presider does this. A congregational hymn is particularly appropriate during this action. The bride and groom remain in a place near the altar. The exact location will depend on the architectural arrangement of the sanctuary. Often they stand together at the liturgical north of the altar.

If incense is used, the presider censes the elements and the altar in the usual way, and the clergy and congregation are censed. The bride and groom are censed with or immediately following those at the altar.

One of the eucharistic prayers that permits the use of the proper preface for marriage is desirable. All may be said or sung according to local custom and the wishes of the participants.

The bride and groom receive communion immediately following the ministers (BCP 432). It is fitting for the presider (or deacon) to hand the chalice to the groom and to permit the couple to communicate each other from it. In some places it is customary for them to assist in communicating the congregation.

Following communion, the proper post-communion prayer is said (BCP 432). The Christian names of the couple are inserted in place of N. and N. in the prayer. If there is a printed program, it is helpful to print the prayer with the names so that everyone may say it together.

There seems little reason to conclude the service with a blessing of the congregation. The nuptial blessing already given is the principal blessing of the service. Following the post-communion prayer, the deacon (or presider) dismisses the people.

g. The Exit
The exit procession is usually led by the bride and groom together, then the best man walking with the maid (or matron) of honor, and the bridesmaids

with the ushers. The liturgical procession may follow, or, more usually, those in the sanctuary exit directly to the sacristy.

If all have entered together in a single liturgical procession, they may exit the same way, with cross and torches leading the procession, then the bride and groom leading the wedding party, and finally the choir, acolytes, and clergy.

b. Weddings at the Sunday Eucharist

It was once common in England for marriages to be held on Sunday mornings, following Morning Prayer and before the eucharist. It was expected that the bride and groom would communicate at the parish eucharist. The practice has been revived in some places, particularly for weddings of active members of the congregation who wish to include the entire parish community in their wedding plans.

It requires a good deal of planning and preparation on the part of the whole congregation, so that they understand that the wedding is a part of the worship life of the community, not an interruption of it for a private service. Such wedding celebrations should be infrequent, lest they disrupt the Sunday cycle, and will more readily find a place in a small closely-knit congregation than in a larger one.

The prayer book does not really address the subject. By analogy to other rites, it would seem that the Sunday propers should be used. If a wedding were held at the Sunday eucharist on the "green Sundays" (that is, the Sundays after Epiphany and Pentecost on which green vestments are traditionally worn) perhaps one or more of the wedding readings could be used, although that is by no means clear. The Sunday color may be used, although many would use white instead of green. Weddings should not normally be held at the Sunday eucharists of Lent or Advent.

Prayers of the people can be written to combine the prayers for the newly married couple with the usual intercessions (BCP 383).

B. The Blessing of a Civil Marriage

This rite is used to bless the marriage of a couple already legally married. Typical uses are with couples who have come to faith since their marriage and wish to have the traditional liturgical blessings added, and with couples whose marriage contracted outside the church has now received ecclesiastical sanction.

The blessing is normally conducted in the context of a eucharist, since the nuptial eucharist is one of the rites people wish to include. This may be done with much of the ceremony of a wedding or quite simply, with only the couple and a few friends present. The blessing could be included in the normal Sunday eucharist by using the propers of the day and adapting the usual prayers of the people to include prayers for the couple.

The couple may enter in procession at the beginning of the service, but more usually they will sit together in the front of the church and come forward after the gospel and homily. The presider addresses them by their Christian names. The husband and wife face each other and respond "I do" to the questions (BCP 433).

The presider asks the congregation to uphold them in their marriage. The wife (and husband) hold out their hands toward the presider, who blesses the rings as they are. The rings may be sprinkled with holy water. The presider joins their right hands and says, "Those whom God has joined together let no one put asunder" (BCP 434).

The service continues as at a wedding, with the prayers and blessing. The couple may return to their places in the congregation or remain near the altar during the eucharistic prayer. They may be a part of the exit procession at the end of the service, or the exit may take place as at a wedding.

C. Anniversary of a Marriage

The Book of Occasional Services contains a form for the renewal of marriage vows on a wedding anniversary (BOS 163-165). It is intended for use at the eucharist. It may be included in a Sunday or holy day service, using the proper of the day. If vows are renewed at a special service, psalms and lessons from the wedding propers may be used. Three alternative collects are given.

Immediately after the sermon (or the creed, if it is said), the husband and wife come from their places in the congregation and stand before the presider, who stands facing the people. The presider addresses the congregation as provided, and asks the man and the woman to renew their marriage vows. They face each other and reply "I do" to the presider's questions. The couple may then kneel, either at the altar rail or some other convenient place provided, or remain standing and say together, "We thank you, gracious God..." (BOS 165).

The presider then blesses the couple. If it is customary, they may be sprinkled with holy water. The service continues with the prayers of the people and the peace. If it is not a principal service, the prayers of the people may be omitted (BOS 165). The couple may bring forward the elements at the offertory.

The Book of Occasional Services also permits the adaptation of this form as an act of reconciliation. The most obvious adaptation would be to alter the presider's opening address along these lines:

> Friends in Christ, we are gathered together with *N.* and *N.*, who have come today to give thanks to God for their reconciliation, to reaffirm their marriage covenant, and to ask God's continued blessing upon their marriage.

The prayer said by the couple can also be altered by adding to the opening petitions a phrase like this:

> We thank you, most gracious God, for reconciling us to each other, and for consecrating our marriage anew in Christ's Name and presence....

3. Reconciliation of a Penitent

The reconciliation of penitents is a not a sacrament of the gospel in the sense that baptism and the eucharist are. The gospels do not show Christ instituting a rite to cover post-baptismal sin. They do, nevertheless, record Christ's commission to the apostles to forgive sin in his name (Matthew 16:19, 18:15, and John 20:22-23; see also 2 Corinthians 5:18-19 for the witness of St. Paul). Like the gospel sacraments, reconciliation is founded on the promise of Christ and the paschal mystery.

> The ministry of reconciliation, which has been committed by Christ to his Church, is exercised through the care each Christian has for others, through the common prayer of Christians assembled for public worship, and through the priesthood of the Church and its ministers declaring absolution.
>
> The Reconciliation of a Penitent is available for all who desire it. It is

not restricted to times of sickness. Confessions may be heard anytime and anywhere. (BCP 446)

In reconciliation the baptismal experience of death to sin and resurrection to newness of life is renewed. Our sins are bound by the love and power of the Crucified One and loosed by our restoration to the risen life in Christ. Reconciliation is an act of Christ in his body the church. The priest hears the confession not only as a minister of Christ, who forgives sin, but also as a representative of the church, the community involved in and injured by the sins of its members.[4]

The opening rubrics of the Reconciliation of a Penitent set the prayer book rite in this context, and establish its general availability "anytime and anywhere" (BCP 446). Traditionally Anglican prayer books have included private confession in the ministry to the sick, but the second rubric makes clear that it is not restricted to that use.

A further rubric states that "the secrecy of a confession is morally absolute for the confessor, and must under no circumstances be broken" (BCP 446). This is the "seal of the confessional" and applies equally to priests and lay confessors.

Since the rite can be celebrated "anytime and anywhere" there is no ceremonial or vesture required. When it is celebrated in the church building, the prayer book recommends that the confessor sit inside the altar rails so that the penitent may kneel at the rail. The confessor should sit either sideways or facing the altar (BCP 446). The traditional vesture is cassock, surplice, and violet stole.

Alternatively, the prayer book suggests "a place set aside to give greater privacy." This may be a traditional confessional in which the priest sits behind a screen and the penitent kneels facing the priest, though there is

---

4. I have discussed the history of the rite of reconciliation in "The Reconciliation of Penitents," in *Anglican Theological Review* 74 (1992), 25-36, and its theology in *Praying Shapes Believing* (Minneapolis: Winston-Seabury Press, 1985; 2nd edition, Wilton,Conn.: Morehouse, 1991), 197-207. Two excellent books on the pastoral and moral theology of hearing confessions are Clark Hyde, *To Declare God's Forgiveness: Toward a Pastoral Theology of Reconciliation* (Wilton, Conn.: Morehouse-Barlow, 1984) and Martin L. Smith, SSJE, *Reconciliation: Preparing for Confession in the Episcopal Church* (Cambridge: Cowley, 1985). Smith's book is written for those making confessions, but it is equally valuable for those hearing confessions.

considerable dissatisfaction with this arrangement. Among other problems, it makes it impossible for the priest to lay hands upon the penitent, the classic outward sign of absolution (BCP 451). A better contemporary plan is a reconciliation room or chapel. This should be a small room where the participants will not be overheard or seen. A sign on the door indicating that the room is in use is helpful. The room should have a crucifix, cross, or icon as a focal center. It might contain a table with an open Bible. It should have a chair for the confessor, a chair facing it for the penitent, and a kneeler near the confessor's chair, so that the penitent may either kneel or sit for a face to face spiritual conference. The room should be well lighted. Copies of *The Book of Common Prayer* or at least the form for the Reconciliation of a Penitent should be available both at the kneeler and at the chair. This will enable the penitent to choose either to kneel or to sit facing the confessor. It is generally a poor idea to hear confessions in the office or study, both because of the danger of interruption and because it tends to equate this with ordinary conversation.

The priest sits in the chair. Some penitents will kneel and begin immediately with the form from the prayer book. Many confessions will begin with the penitent choosing to sit opposite the confessor and converse informally. The confessor helps the penitent to identify and name sins, and together they gain a picture of the penitent's spiritual state. This may eventuate in the penitent using one of the two forms and receiving absolution, or it may result simply in the penitent naming and confessing sins, after which the absolution is pronounced.

It is important to note that for the legal protection of the priest the forms from *The Book of Common Prayer* must be used, so that the conversation is clearly a confession and not simply a pastoral consultation. The distinction may be important in law if a priest is called to testify concerning what was said. Often lay confessors are not protected by law, although they are bound by the "seal." Since state laws and diocesan interpretations of the laws vary, confessors should ascertain what the legal situation is in their jurisdiction.

Whether or not the confession has been preceded by a spiritual conference, the formal liturgical act begins with the use of one of the two forms from the prayer book. The penitent may sit or kneel. The confessor sits.

A. Form One

Form One previously has been commonly used by Anglicans, although it has not appeared in *The Book of Common Prayer*. The penitent begins, "Bless me, for I have sinned." The priest gives the blessing, making the sign of the cross over (or toward) the penitent. The penitent then says, "I confess to Almighty God, to his Church, and to you, that...," inserting the sins being confessed after "especially" (BCP 447).

When the penitent completes the form, the priest gives such council, direction, and comfort as seems appropriate. As a rule of thumb, if the confessor has nothing in particular to say, it is better to say nothing. If there has not been conversation before the confession, a conversation may take some time. The confessor assigns the penitent a penance: "a psalm, prayer, or hymn to be said, or something to be done, as a sign of penitence and act of thanksgiving" (BCP 446). The penance should be something that can be said or done immediately, or in a short time, not a long-term program for improvement. It is not intended to be a condition of absolution or an act of satisfaction. Forgiveness is the free gift of God. There is nothing human beings can do to earn forgiveness or to atone for sin. All that can be done has been done by Christ's "one oblation of himself once offered...for the sins of the whole world" (BCP 334). We can only accept with thanksgiving and penitence the unmerited gift of which the penance is the sign.

Once the penitent has indicated that the counsel is understood and the penance accepted, the priest pronounces absolution. Either form may be used (BCP 448). If it can conveniently be done, the priest may stand and lay a hand on the head of the penitent. The priest may make the sign of the cross at the words "absolve you."

The priest then adds "The Lord has put away all your sins," and the dismissal (BCP 448). The penitent leaves the place where the confession has been heard and performs the penance as soon as possible. If the penitent is to remain where the confession was heard, the priest substitutes "abide" for "go" in the dismissal.

B. Form Two

Form Two was written for the 1979 prayer book and is influenced by Eastern Orthodox forms. It sets the forgiveness of sins in the baptismal framework and uses the image of the prodigal son (Luke 15:11-32). The form provides a richer theological context for reconciliation, but it is longer and requires more responses from the penitent.

The priest and penitent begin by saying together a portion of Psalm 51, the classic penitential psalm (BCP 449). The penitent then says, "Pray for me, a sinner." The priest pronounces the blessing, making a cross over the penitent. The priest then says the comfortable words, or some other appropriate verses of scripture. These words were chosen for the rite because of their familiarity to many Episcopalians through their inclusion in the Rite I eucharist (BCP 332), but today fewer penitents find the passages familiar, and some are offended by their use of "men" and "man" to refer to people of both sexes. The use of a different translation or other passages will solve the problem.

The priest then invites the penitent to confess his or her sins, "in the presence of Christ, and of me, his minister" (BCP 450). The penitent recites the form of confession, mentioning particular sins after "Especially, I confess to you and to the Church...."

The priest then gives counsel, direction, and comfort as described above and assigns a penance. This conversation may take some time. When it is completed the priest asks the penitent, "Will you turn again to Christ as your Lord?" and "Do you, then, forgive those who have sinned against you?" and says the prayer following.

The priest then stands (if it is convenient) and lays a hand on the head of the penitent, saying the absolution. Either form may be used. If it is impossible to lay a hand on the head of the penitent, the priest may extend a hand toward the penitent (BCP 451). The priest may make the sign of the cross at "absolve you."

The priest dismisses the penitent saying, "Now there is rejoicing in heaven." The penitent leaves to perform the penance. If the penitent is not to leave, the priest substitutes "abide" for "go" in the dismissal.

C. Lay Confessors

The Book of Common Prayer permits a lay Christian to hear a confession, but he or she must make clear that absolution will not be pronounced. This provision is in accord with Christian tradition. Its most obvious uses are in cases of genuine emergency when a priest in unavailable, and in the course of spiritual direction by a lay spiritual director. In the second case, the confession may have much of the liturgical formality described above and come at the conclusion of extended spiritual conference.

A lay confessor does not make the sign of the cross over the penitent and substitutes the declaration of forgiveness (BCP 448, 452) for the absolution Form Two is probably better suited for the use of a lay confessor, and if Form One is used the prayer "May God in his love enlighten your heart" (BCP 449) from Form Two may replace the more declarative form "The Lord be in your heart" (BCP 447).

A lay confessor is bound by "the seal of the confessional" just as a priest is.

4. Christian Service

The Book of Common Prayer contains A Form of Commitment to Christian Service (BCP 420-421). This form was prepared originally by the committee that drafted *Prayer Book Studies 18* on Christian initiation for persons who wished "to make or renew a commitment to the service of Christ in the world, either in general terms, or upon undertaking some special responsibility" (BCP 420). Similarly, a Commissioning for Lay Ministries in the Church can be found in *The Book of Occasional Services,* which notes:

> The Ministers of the Church are lay persons, bishops, priests, and deacons. Lay persons are commissioned for their ministry by the Sacrament of Holy Baptism, and no form of commissioning for special functions is necessary. (BOS 179)

This comment applies equally to the Commitment to Christian Service. In other words, the rationale for all these rites is pastoral. They are not intended to authorize anyone to exercise a ministry, but to publicly recognize that they are already exercising it.

The principal difference between the two rites is that the rite in *The Book of Occasional Services* is concerned with "churchy" ministries: vestry members, deputies to convention, servers, altar guild members, teachers, evangelists, singers, church musicians, lectors, ministers of communion, lay readers, parish visitors, canvassers, prayer group members, and officers of parish organizations. The form in *The Book of Common Prayer* has the wider perspective of ministry in the world, which we often neglect to consider as Christian ministry. Suggestions that have been made for its use are beginning study, entering a profession, retiring, or simply a renewed commitment to seeing life as ministry.

The renewal of baptismal vows in the prayer book rite is intended to underline the fact that it is baptism which commissions us to be ministers of Christ. It is important that the rite be used to "strengthen us all in our Christian vocation of witness to the world, and of service to others" (BCP 421), rather than to suggest that such service is an optional extra for a committed few.

There is some obvious overlap between this and the reaffirmation rite associated with confirmation. This rite was seen by its compilers as more informal, not requiring the presence of the bishop, and giving people an opportunity to express their commitment in their own words.

A. A Form of Commitment to Christian Service

The actual rite is quite simple. After the prayers of the people at the eucharist, the presider invites the person making the commitment to come forward. That person, "standing before the congregation, makes the Act of Commitment" (BCP 420). This act is prepared beforehand by the person in consultation with the presider. It may be either a statement of intention or a series of questions to which the person responds. In either case, it includes a reaffirmation of baptismal promises (BCP 420). A simple way to do this would be to have the person read a statement of his or her intentions, describing the service of Christ in the world to that the commitment refers, and then use the renewal of baptismal promises from the Easter Vigil, concluding with the collect appointed (BCP 421).

The presider may then add any appropriate prayers for the work that the person is undertaking, such as those in the Prayers and Thanksgiving section of *The Book of Common Prayer*. The eucharist then continues with the exchange of the peace and the offertory.

B. Commissioning for Lay Ministries in the Church

The rite takes place following the homily and creed at the eucharist, or at the time of the hymn or anthem following the collects at Morning or Evening Prayer. It may also stand alone (BOS 180). Most frequently it will be used at the Sunday eucharist. A churchwarden or other suitable representative of the congregation is appointed as sponsor of the candidates. If there are different groups being commissioned, each group is presented separately.

The congregation are seated. If the rector is not the presider of the eucharist, it is nevertheless appropriate for the rector or priest-in-charge to preside at this rite. The presider moves to a place "in full view of the people." This may be standing in front of the altar, or at a lectern with a microphone. The candidates and sponsor(s) come forward. The presider reads the introduction, "Brothers and Sister in Christ Jesus, we are all baptized by the one Spirit" (BOS 180) and asks the sponsor if the persons are prepared to exercise their ministries (BOS 181).

The sponsor responds and the presider addresses the candidates, who respond, "I will." If the rite is being conducted as a separate service, a scripture reading from the list on page 195 of *The Book of Occasional Services* and a homily follow.

Separate commissioning for sixteen different ministries is included (BOS 182-195). Seldom will more than one or two be used at the same service. Each group is presented and commissioned separately. The form for each group is parallel.

The sponsor presents the candidates, using the form in *The Book of Occasional Services* for the appropriate group. The antiphon may be sung by the choir, but more usually it will be said by those present. The presider (or a cantor) says (or sings) the versicle (V.) and all respond (R.). The presider, with hands in the orans position (unless holding a book), says "Let us pray," and after a pause for silent prayer, says (or sings) the collect appointed. The presider then says to each person the sentence of commissioning ("In the name of God and of this congregation, I commission you") and gives to each an appropriate symbol of ministry. If the number of persons is large, the sentence may be said only once, but each person is greeted and given a symbol.

No suggestions are made in *The Book of Occasional Services* as to what symbols are appropriate. It some cases the answer is obvious. A lector could receive a Bible, a lay reader a prayer book, and a singer a hymnal, but in many cases the service gives the parish an opportunity to think creatively.

If the commissioning is held at the eucharist, the service continues with the prayers of the people and the peace. A collect for optional use at the conclusion of the prayers is included (BOS 195). At the daily office the prayer and the peace are used to conclude the rite. When the commissioning stands alone, the prayer, the Lord's Prayer, the peace, and a blessing conclude the service.

5. Celebration for a Home

The Celebration for a Home, or house blessing, has become one of the most popular services in *The Book of Occasional Services*. It is used, sometimes quite formally, to bless monasteries and rectories, and informally for blessing the homes of ordinary Christians. The blessing may include a celebration of the eucharist in the home. If there is a chapel in the house, the eucharist is celebrated there, but most frequently it will be a "house mass" celebrated in the living room or dining room. A table is prepared there for the celebration of the eucharist, with bread, wine, water, a plate, and a chalice or glass. A purificator (or other cloth to wipe the cup) is needed and a corporal (or tablecloth) is placed under the vessels.

A. The Full Service

The family and friends gather in the living room with the priest. The priest may vest in cassock and surplice or alb and stole (either white or the color of the day), but unless the blessing is quite formal, the priest usually wears ordinary clothes.

The priest greets the people with "The Lord be with you" and says an opening collect. One is printed in the service, but "some other appropriate collect" may be substituted (BOS 146).

One or two lessons are read by members of the family or by friends. The readers stand. Everyone else sits wherever it is convenient. Genesis 18:1-8 and 3 John 1-6a, 13-15 are appointed as lessons, but other choices are permitted. Psalm 112:1-7 "or some other psalm or song" follows the first reading. The psalm may be read or sung responsively or in unison, or something suitable may be sung.

If the eucharist is to be celebrated, the gospel reading is always included. John 11:5 and 12:1-3 or Matthew 6:25-33 are recommended. The priest, or a deacon if one is present, reads the gospel with the usual announcement and conclusion. All stand for the gospel. Someone may give a brief address.

The priest then stands and says the invocation with hands extended, "Let the mighty power of the Holy God be present in this place..." (BOS 147).

A member of the family carrying a lighted candle then leads the procession from room to room around the house. In a formal blessing—of a religious house, for example—a crucifer and torches may lead the procession. In each room the appointed antiphon, versicle and response, and collect are said. This may be done in any convenient order. The antiphons may be sung, but will usually be recited aloud by the priest. Someone else may lead the antiphon and say (or sing) the versicles. If copies of the service are available to the people, they may join in saying (or singing) the antiphons, and make the responses to the versicles. The priest says (or sings) the collects and may sprinkle each room with holy water, either during the antiphon or at the conclusion of the collect.

Verses of hymns may be sung as the procession moves from room to room. When all rooms have been visited, the procession returns to the living room. The antiphon, versicle, and collect for the blessing of the home are said. The priest may sprinkle the room and the people with holy water. The peace is exchanged.

If the eucharist is not celebrated, the service concludes with the Lord's Prayer and a blessing. *The Book of Occasional Services* urges that if the eucharist is not celebrated at this time, it be celebrated in the house as soon as convenient (BOS 156).

The priest goes to the table. The people stand around the table. If the bread and wine are not already on the table they are brought to it by members of the family. The priest (or a deacon) sets the table, placing bread on the plate or paten and wine and water in the glass or chalice.

The priest recites one of the eucharistic prayers. If it is a prayer that may include a proper preface, the one on page 155 of *The Book of Occasional Services* can be used.

The priest may administer communion either by going from person to person or standing by the table and having everyone come by. Another authorized eucharistic minister may administer the cup. Alternatively, the priest may administer the bread to the closest person, who then administers it to the next person, continuing around the room, and then do the same with the wine. This conforms to the rubric in An Order for

Celebrating the Holy Eucharist, "The Body and Blood of the Lord are shared in a reverent manner" (BCP 401), and is probably the best method to use in a home if there is no one to administer the cup.

A proper post-communion prayer may be used (BOS 156). The service concludes with a dismissal. Refreshments may be served following the blessing.

B. A Shorter Version

The service may be shortened by (a) using fewer readings, (b) omitting the procession through the rooms, and (c) omitting the eucharist. In its shortest form, all gather in the living room. The priest says the salutation and opening collect, a single passage from scripture is read, followed by the antiphon, versicle, and collect for the blessing (BOS 154-155). The priest may then sprinkle the house and the people with holy water, and all exchange the peace. All say the Lord's Prayer together, and the priest gives a blessing.

6. Ministry to the Sick and Dying

The Ministration to the Sick in *The Book of Common Prayer* is an expression of the healing ministry of Jesus Christ, which the apostles exercised in his name. This ministry is a part of the mission of the Christian church. Its theological thrust is precisely healing. The prayer for blessing the oil for anointing the sick prays that "as your holy apostles anointed many that were sick and healed them, so may those who in faith and repentance receive this holy unction be made whole" (BCP 455). Inherited medieval forms in earlier prayer books tended to pray for grace to accept sickness and die well, while anointing had become "extreme unction" and the whole ministration "last rites." The 1979 *Book of Common Prayer* returns to the emphasis on healing, continuing the movement in this direction begun in 1928.

The 1979 prayer book has also tried to avoid the opposite error of not taking seriously the possibility that the sick person may die, especially since our society often is unwilling to face the fact of death. Ministration at the Time of Death is thus in a separate section, recognizing that we all shall die and that some sick people will not recover, but avoiding the suggestion that only those who are dying should receive the ministrations of the church, or that the priest should only be called when the doctors have given up hope.

An adaptation of the anointing and laying on of hands for use in church, called A Public Service of Healing, is included in *The Book of Occasional Services* (BOS 166-173).

A. Ministration to the Sick

The service in *The Book of Common Prayer* (BCP 453-461) contains a number of parts, which will probably not all be used at the same time. They represent the major ministries to the sick, and if more than one is used they follow in the order printed. Although these ministries are liturgical as well as pastoral they are normally used in the sickroom and not in the church.

Traditions vary concerning vesture for the ministration of the sick. In some places, a priest making a formal sick call wears cassock, surplice, and stole, but usually the visitor wears ordinary clothes. Often a priest or deacon will wear a white stole for administering communion, and a violet stole for anointing and for hearing confessions. Ribbon stoles for wear with normal attire, reversible violet and white, are quite common, although many clergy consider them unnecessary and will wear either a full stole or none at all. Lay persons engaged in this ministry normally wear their own clothes.

The traditional greeting, "Peace be to this house (place), and to all who dwell in it" (BCP 453) is an excellent way for a minister, lay or ordained, making a formal sick call to begin.

a. Ministry of the Word

Reading the Bible to the sick is a Christian ministry that any Christian able to read aloud may exercise. *The Book of Common Prayer* suggests appropriate readings, and the possibility of the reader commenting on any passage. Other passages may be used. Suggestions are made for appropriate readings for penitence, anointing, and communion. Lay eucharistic ministers, deacons, or priests bringing communion to the sick may use one or more of those readings, or the propers of the day. Care should be taken not to tire the sick person, although the bedridden and chronically ill may wish to hear all of the Sunday readings. Some places record portions of the

Sunday liturgy, including music, for visitors to play when visiting the sick at home or in nursing homes.

The reading of scripture is the normal beginning of other ministrations, although it may be omitted if the patient is seriously ill. It may also stand alone, concluding with the Lord's Prayer or other suitable prayers.

b. Special Confession

> The priest may suggest the making of a special confession, if the sick person's conscience is troubled, and use the form for the Reconciliation of a Penitent. (BCP 454)

Confession is not listed as a separate part of the ministration by *The Book of Common Prayer,* but this rubric, based on that in 1549 and subsequent prayer books, is the classic place where the making of a private confession has appeared in Anglican liturgy. If the sick person wishes to make a confession, the priest asks other people present to leave temporarily. If the minister is not a priest, he or she must tell that to the sick person and follow the directions for deacons and lay persons (BCP 446).

If the sick person does not wish to make a special confession, the general confession may be used (BCP 454). If the visitor is not a priest the usual alterations are made in the absolution (BCP 455). The general confession is especially appropriate before anointing or communion.

c. Laying on of Hands and Anointing

The oil for the anointing of the sick may be blessed by the bishop or a priest. It is most convenient if blessed oil is kept in the church and brought to the place where it is to be used in an oil stock. A small oil stock is filled with absorbent cotton and the blessed oil poured over it. The anointer may then place the thumb against the cotton and mark the cross on the forehead of the sick person.

If no blessed oil is available, the priest blesses pure olive oil, using the form on page 455 of *The Book of Common Prayer.* The oil may be blessed in a bottle with a stopper or screw top and a small amount poured into the oil stock. The priest says the prayer with hands in the orans position, either extending them over the oil or making the sign of the cross over the oil at the words, "Send your Holy Spirit to sanctify this oil." The blessing may be done in the sick room or at a public healing service in the church. The blessed oil is kept at the church for future use.

The anointing follows the confession and absolution. The anthem "Savior of the world" is said and the priest lays hands upon the sick person. The first of the two forms in *The Book of Common Prayer* includes the phrase "to drive away all sickness of body and spirit"; the second prays "that you may know the healing power of [Christ's] love" (BCP 456). The priest must decide which is more appropriate.

The priest then anoints the sick person, making the sign of the cross on his or her forehead with the oil, placing the thumb against the oil-soaked cotton in the oil stock and marking the cross with the thumb, as described above. The priest may add the following prayer:

> As you are outwardly anointed with this holy oil, so may our heavenly Father grant you the inward anointing of the Holy Spirit. Of his great mercy, may he forgive you your sins, release you from suffering, and restore you to wholeness and strength. May he deliver you from all evil, preserve you in all goodness, and bring you to everlasting life; through Jesus Christ our Lord. Amen. (BCP 456)

This prayer, originally from the 1549 prayer book, is an excellent theological summary of the meaning of the anointing. It is worth using if the sick person is able to understand what is being said, or if there are others present who would be helped by hearing it.

If communion is be administered, the blessing "The Almighty Lord, who is a strong tower" follows the anointing at once; otherwise, the ministration concludes with the Lord's Prayer and that blessing (BCP 456-457). This blessing is an appropriate conclusion to any visit to a sick person, and if it had not already been done, the priest may lay a hand on the sick person while saying it.

d. Holy Communion

Communion of the sick may take the form either of a celebration of the eucharist or ministration from the reserved sacrament. Lay eucharistic ministers, priests, bishops, or deacons may bring the reserved sacrament to the sick from the Sunday eucharist. *The Book of Common Prayer* specifically recommends a celebration for those who are regularly unable to attend church:

When persons are unable to be present for extended periods, it is desirable that the priest arrange to celebrate the Eucharist with them from time to time on a regular basis, using either the Proper of the Day or one of those appointed for Various Occasions. (BCP 396)

At other times communion may be from the reserved sacrament (BCP 396). This is the best way to communicate those acutely ill. Taking the reserved sacrament directly from the parish eucharist to the sick person is a means of inclusion in the parish celebration. Separate rubrics permit a sick person unable to receive either the bread or wine to receive communion in one kind (BCP 457) and assure those unable to receive in either kind "that all the benefits of Communion are received, even though the Sacrament is not received with the mouth" (BCP 457). "It is desirable that fellow parishioners, relatives, and friends be present, when possible, to communicate with them" (BCP 396).

i. Eucharist in the Sick Room

If the eucharist is to be celebrated in the sick room, the priest will need a table to use as an altar. Also needed are a corporal or other cloth to place on the table under the vessels, a chalice or glass, a paten or plate to hold the bread, wine, water, and a copy of *The Book of Common Prayer* or the necessary portions thereof. A portable communion set will contain the items needed in a carrying case. Frequently a cross, screw-top cruets, purificator, stole, and other helpful items will be included. The use of the tiny vessels in some older communion sets is to be avoided. Not only do they suggest "playing church," but they are difficult to handle and use, especially for a person confined to bed.

The Ministry of the Word takes place, as above, then the celebration continues with the peace and the offertory. If the person is acutely ill, it is preferable to administer communion from the reserved sacrament, but if it seems desirable, the eucharist may be celebrated beginning with the offertory, omitting or abbreviating the Ministry of the Word.

If the visit is a scheduled celebration for someone who is shut-in, the celebration should be as full as possible. The priest may wear vestments and use the propers of the day or those For the Sick from Various Occasions in *The Book of Common Prayer* (BCP 931). It may be desirable to use the full form of the service, whether Rite One or Rite Two, to which the sick person is accustomed. The service may easily be shortened by following the directions in An Order for Celebrating the Holy Eucharist (BCP 400-401).

A typical service for someone who is shut-in would begin with the priest arranging the vessels on the table and putting on a stole, or eucharistic vestments as appropriate. The service can begin with "The Lord be with you," a collect, and the readings. It is desirable that someone other than the priest read the first (and second) lesson. Some who are shut-in are willing and able to read the lessons themselves. If no one else is able to do so, the priest may read them. The priest reads the gospel, unless a deacon is present. The priest or someone else leads a brief form of the prayers of the people, preferably one not requiring a book for responses. If the confession of sin has not be said earlier, it follows. The priest says the absolution.

Whether only the eucharist is celebrated or it follows after the earlier parts of the Ministration to the Sick, the peace may now be exchanged. If the vessels have not been arranged on the table, that is done now. The priest places bread on the paten and wine and water in the chalice and stands at the table facing the sick person. The other people present may stand or sit as convenient. Any of the authorized eucharistic prayers may be used. In most cases minimal ceremonial is desirable: ceremonial actions that are fitting in a church often seem exaggerated and out of place in a more informal setting. All say the Lord's Prayer together. The priest breaks the bread, says "The gifts of God for the people of God," receives communion, and administers communion to the sick person(s), and then to the others present. Any of the consecrated gifts that remain are consumed or taken back to the church to be reserved.

A proper post-communion prayer may be used (BCP 457), or one of those usually used at public celebrations may be said. The service concludes with a blessing or dismissal.

ii. Communion from the Reserved Sacrament

If a bishop, priest, or deacon brings the reserved sacrament from the church, the prayer book form Communion under Special Circumstances (BCP 396) is used. When lay eucharistic ministers bring the reserved sacrament, the Distribution of Holy Communion by Lay Eucharistic Ministers from *The Book of Occasional Services* (BOS 227-228), as described in the following section, is used.

The sacrament is reserved in the church in an aumbry or tabernacle. Leavened bread may be reserved for administration within a day or two following the parish eucharist, but for continuous reservation for use in emergencies it is often more convenient to reserve wafer bread, since leavened bread will become stale. Wine is reserved in a cruet with a stopper. It should be renewed weekly.

The consecrated bread is carried in a pyx or bread box that closes tightly. If communion is brought in both kinds, the consecrated wine is carried in a screw-top cruet or small bottle and poured into a chalice for administering. An alternative method, particularly useful if it is difficult to carry the consecrated wine to the sick person, is to intinct the bread before leaving the church. This should be done carefully so as not to make the bread soggy. An efficient way to accomplish this is simply to touch a small piece of intincted bread to the center of the host and pack it away.

In some places the minister carries the sacrament from the church wearing vestments, usually cassock, surplice, and stole, or alb and stole, but more usually ordinary clothes are worn. A stole may be worn during the service, but many feel it is better to wear either full vestments or none.

If a suitable table is available, the minister sets down the pyx or communion set, spreading a corporal or some other suitable cloth under it. If communion is to be administered in both kinds, the wine is poured into a chalice and set upon the table.

If none of the previous sections of the Ministration of the Sick have been used, a passage from scripture is read and may be commented on briefly (BCP 397). The minister then offers "suitable prayers," concluding with a collect. A suggested collect is on page 397 of *The Book of Common Prayer*. The confession of sin may follow. The form most familiar to the sick person is the best choice. The minister, if a priest, says the absolution. A deacon makes the customary changes in the form (BCP 398).

If the Ministry of the Word (and other sections) from the Ministration to the Sick have been used, then the administration of communion begins with the peace and the Lord's Prayer (BCP 457).

The minister opens the pyx, picks up the bread, and, if wine is used, holds it over the cup of wine, saying, "The Gifts of God for the people of God." The sick person receives communion first, then others who are also receiving. The usual words of administration are used. If communion is in one kind or by intinction, it may be helpful to give the sick person a drink of water to help him or her swallow.

Either one of the usual post-communion prayers or the special one provided may be used (BCP 399, 457). The service concludes with a blessing or dismissal.

Any consecrated elements left over are returned to the church or consumed.

iii. Distribution of Communion by Lay Eucharistic Ministers

The Book of Occasional Services contains a special form for the Distribution of Holy Communion by Lay Eucharistic Ministers to persons who are ill or infirm (BOS 226-230). This distribution is limited to what is called "extended communion," that is, taking the sacrament directly from the parish celebration to the persons to receive. This communion is an extension of the distribution to those present at the eucharist and includes the sick or infirm member in the action of the congregation. Other members of the congregation should accompany the lay eucharistic minister.

Following the communion of the people at the service in church, the lay eucharistic ministers come forward. The presider commends their ministry to the congregation, saying:

> In the name of this congregation, I send you forth bearing these holy gifts, that those to whom you go may share with us in the communion of Christ's body and blood. We who are many are one body, because we all share one bread, one cup. (BOS 229)

The presider may substitute "similar words." Each minister is given a container with consecrated bread and wine, corporal, and purificator. The deacon (or the presider, or an assisting priest) places the consecrated bread and wine in the containers at the time of communion, so that they are ready to give to the eucharistic ministers when they come forward. The lay eucharistic ministers depart to administer communion to the absent.

When the minister arrives at the place where communion is to be distributed, the communion set is placed on a convenient table. The corporal is spread and the bread and wine placed upon it. If communion is to be administered in both kinds, the wine is poured into the chalice provided. Since it is difficult to pour wine back into a cruet or bottle, the minister should not pour out more wine than will be needed. The eucharistic minister then greets the people saying, "The Peace of the Lord be always with you," to which all respond, "And also with you" (BOS 227). The minister reads the collect of the day facing the sick person, holding the book in both hands. The eucharistic minister, or one of the people accompanying the minister, reads the gospel of the day, or some other passage of scripture. On Ascension and Pentecost, for example, the reading from Acts might be read rather than the gospel. An appropriate reading from those given in the Ministration to the Sick is another possible substitute. Comments on the sermon of the day may be made. Some congregations play taped portions of the service and sermon at this point, but care must be taken not to tire the sick person by doing too much.

Suitable prayers, such as those for the sick, may be offered. The confession of sin is usually said. It may be omitted, but it is ordinarily a part of the distribution of communion to the sick. A form for the lay minister to use instead of the absolution is in *The Book of Occasional Services*:

May Almighty God in mercy receive our confession of sorrow and faith, strengthen us in all goodness, and by the power of the Holy Spirit keep us in eternal life. (BOS 228)

The minister leads those present in the Lord's Prayer. Either the traditional or contemporary form may be used, but it is best to use the form to which the sick person is more accustomed. The minister distributes communion to the sick person, using the accustomed words. A closing prayer is given in *The Book of Occasional Services* (BOS 228), after which the minister concludes the service with the dismissal, "Let us bless the Lord."

The minister returns the vessels and the unused bread and wine to the container, and either continues to the next place where communion is to be distributed or returns everything to the church. The minister and those present may consume small amounts of leftover bread and wine, but any substantive amounts should be returned to the church to be reserved for other communions.

B. A Public Service of Healing

This service from *The Book of Occasional Services* (BOS 166-173) is an adaptation of the rite for anointing and laying on of hands in *The Book of Common Prayer* for use in church as a public service—a widespread practice throughout the church today.

The service is a part of a eucharistic celebration. The propers may be those of the day, or chosen from a table in *The Book of Occasional Services* (BOS 171-173). The table is quite extensive, offering a number of options. If the service is a part of a Sunday or major holy day celebration, the propers will normally be those of the day. Some congregations, for example, celebrate St. Luke's Day, or the patronal festival of a diocesan hospital, with a public service of healing. On other occasions, readings and psalms from the table will usually be chosen. A collect for use with the psalms and lesson is included in the service (BOS 166). The collect of the day or another suitable collect may be used instead.

If the propers of the day are used, the color is that of the day. Otherwise the color may be that of the day or violet. The service may begin with the penitential order, or the confession of sin may follow the Litany of Healing (BOS 166, 169).

A Litany of Healing (BOS 167) may replace the prayers of the people. If it is a Sunday or major holy day service, more general petitions may be included. The celebrant introduces the litany, standing at the chair and facing the people, with "Let us name before God those for whom we offer our prayers." The people are encouraged to name audibly those for whom they are interceding. This is the place at which the names of people not present for whom we wish to pray, as well as those who are present seeking healing, may be said aloud.

A deacon or other person appointed leads the litany. The presider concludes the litany with one of the three collects given, or some other suitable collect (BOS 169). If the penitential order did not begin the service, the confession of sin follows. The deacon (or the presider) says the invitation, and following the confession the presider (or the bishop) faces the people and says the absolution, making the sign of the cross over the people. A server may hold the book.

If oil for the sick is to be blessed it is done now by the presider (or the bishop, if present), using the form in *The Book of Common Prayer* (BCP 455). The oil may be in oil stocks or in a glass bottle. It is easiest if the oil to be used during the service is already in oil stocks set out open to be blessed, but it is more effective visually if a bottle of olive oil is blessed and the oil then poured into the oil stocks for use. If the bishop is the presider, it is fitting for the bishop to bless sufficient oil for use during the year. The oil to be blessed is held by a server or placed on a small table. The presider stands facing the people and says the prayer with hands in the orans position, either extending them over the oil or making the sign of the cross over the oil at the words, "Send your Holy Spirit to sanctify this oil." At the conclusion of the prayer, the oil is placed in oil stocks or other vessels and given to the priests who will perform the anointing. Oil not used at the service is kept for future use.

If the oil is already blessed, a server brings oil stocks from the credence table to the presider and any priests who will assist in the anointing at this time.

The presider then invites those who wish to receive the laying on of hands and anointing to come forward (BOS 169). The anthem "Savior of the world" may be sung or said while they are coming forward. The presider, standing in front of the altar facing the people who have come forward, says, with hands extended toward them, the blessing, "The Almighty Lord, who is a strong tower" (BCP 456, BOS 170). If there are many persons to receive the anointing and laying on of hands, other priests may assist in the anointing. Each will need an oil stock.

The priests lay hands on each person, and mark a cross on the forehead with their thumbs, having dipped their thumbs in the oil (BOS 170). The forms printed in *The Book of Occasional Services* need not be used, and each person may be prayed for individually according to his or her needs. The anointing may also be omitted, and only the laying on of hands and signing with the cross used.

The forms all call for the person to be healed to be prayed for by name. People coming forward may be told to say their name to the priest so that it can be used.

A rubric states that "lay persons with a gift of healing may join the celebrant in the laying on of hands" (BOS 170). No criteria are provided for determining who such persons are. They may be members of the Order of St. Luke or other healing fellowships, or others who have this gift. Presumably this means that such persons may join with the priest in laying on hands, not that they may lay hands on some while the priest lays hands on others. If there are many such people they may accompany each of the priests laying on hands and anointing. They may place their hands on the head or shoulders of the persons asking for healing along with the priest.

The people may kneel at the altar rail as those laying on hands move along the rail, or the people may come to one or more stations before the altar where those laying on hands and anointing will wait for them.

After all who desire it have received the laying on of hands, those who have done the anointing wash their hands. Water and lemon juice (or liquid soap) are effective for removing the oil. The presider then greets the people, inviting them to exchange the peace (BOS 171).

If the service is not a eucharistic celebration, it concludes with the Lord's Prayer and a special prayer and blessing (BOS 171). Otherwise, it continues with the offertory.

After communion, a special prayer replaces the usual post-communion prayer (BOS 171) and the presider pronounces a special blessing. The service concludes with the dismissal by the deacon, or the presider.

C. Ministration at the Time of Death

The Book of Common Prayer contains a separate section for Ministration at the Time of Death (BCP 462-467). The rites included in the Ministration to the Sick are, of course, also suitably administered to the dying. Confession, anointing, and communion are particularly appropriate, and if they are used with a dying person, they precede the ministry at time of death. Obviously, the person must be conscious to make a confession or to receive communion. Anointing and laying on of hands can be administered to an unconscious person, whether or not that person is expected to recover. Clearly, the ministry to the sick should not be postponed until the person is near death.

The specific ministrations for the dying are a Litany at the Time of Death (which may also be used after the person has died), and three prayers. The litany, based on the Sarum litany for the dying, is a responsive prayer that may be said with family members when a person is dying. Often the family members are anxious to have something useful to do, and joining in the litany is helpful to them. There are occasions when it is appropriately said with the sick person. My father asked me to say the Litany at the Time of Death with him the last time I saw him alive.

A Prayer for a Person near Death (BCP 462) is appropriate, with or without the litany. A Commendation at the Time of Death (BCP 464), also based on that in the Sarum *Manuale,* is intended to be said as the person dies. A Commendatory Prayer (BCP 465) may be said after the person has died.

If the priest arrives after the person has died, the litany and commendatory prayer are still appropriate, especially as prayers with the family. The commendation may be said if the body is still present.

The Prayers for a Vigil and Reception of the Body (BCP 465-467), included in this section in *The Book of Common Prayer,* are treated under the heading The Burial of the Dead below.

7. The Burial of the Dead

The Book of Common Prayer contains three rites for the Burial of the Dead, Rites One and Two and An Order for Burial. In addition, forms for a vigil or wake and the reception of the body are included in the Ministration at Time of Death. *The Book of Occasional Services* contains a Burial of One Who Does Not Profess the Christian Faith (BOS 175-178) for use with An Order for Burial (BCP 506-507).

During the Middle Ages Christian burial rites tended to focus on the Last Judgment and pray that the souls of the departed be delivered from hell and eternal damnation. This mindset survived the Reformation. The 1979 *Book of Common Prayer,* however, affirms forcefully that "the liturgy for the dead is an Easter liturgy":

> It finds its meaning in the resurrection. Because Jesus was raised from the dead, we, too, shall be raised. The liturgy, therefore is characterized by joy, in the certainty that "neither death, nor life, nor angels, nor powers, nor height, nor depth, nor anything else in all creation, will be able to separate us from the love of God in Christ Jesus our Lord." (BCP 507)

Although this joy is tempered by our sorrow in separation from those we love, it is still the primary character of the funeral liturgy. Its tone is perhaps best expressed by the *contakion* from the Russian liturgy that is a part of the

Commendation. "All of us go down to the dust; yet even at the grave we make our song: Alleluia, alleluia, alleluia" (BCP 499).

The medieval liturgy of the dead consisted of a procession with the body to the church, an office (*Dirige* or Dirge) and a mass (*Requiem*), and a committal. The 1549 prayer book provided both for a burial office and a celebration of the eucharist. The propers for the eucharist were dropped in 1552, and only the office remained. The eucharistic propers reappeared in the American prayer book of 1928.

The burial rite in the 1979 *Book of Common Prayer* is set in the context of a eucharistic Word liturgy. No provision is made for an office of the dead, but if it is desired, either as a part of the vigil or as a memorial service, psalms, lessons, and collects such as those in the burial service can be used with appropriate canticles. The prayers of the people from the burial service might replace the suffrages.

The prayer book assumes that Christians will be buried from the church, that the service will be held at a time when the congregation can be present, and that the arrangements have been made in consultation with the parish priest (BCP 468, 490). It is helpful in accomplishing all this if (a) parish clergy have good working relationships with undertakers, (b) dioceses and parishes have published guidelines concerning funerals, and (c) clergy have taught parishioners about what is done and why.

Usually the body is brought to the church for the funeral; the coffin is closed before the funeral and not opened again (BCP 468, 490). Burial or cremation takes place following the service, accompanied by a service of committal. The committal may also take place before the funeral. This is customary in tropical countries where burials are held as soon as possible, and funeral services follow.

Since the funeral liturgy is an Easter liturgy, white vestments are usually worn. The older tradition of wearing black vestments is to be discouraged. During Lent the Lenten array may be left in place during the funeral, but the liturgy remains an Easter liturgy, and "Alleluia" is sung where it occurs in the rite.

A bishop or priest normally presides at a funeral, but if none is available, a deacon or lay reader may preside. The bishop, if present, normally presides at the eucharist and the commendation (BCP 490). The eucharist may be celebrated at the funeral of any baptized Christian, and its celebration at the funerals of communicants of the Episcopal Church is encouraged. The celebration of the eucharist at the burial of Christians is the oldest Christian burial rite of which we know, as recorded in the *Didascalia Apostolorum:*

> Come together even in the cemeteries, and read the holy Scriptures, and without demur perform your ministry and your supplication to God; and offer an acceptable Eucharist, the likeness of the royal body of Christ, both in your congregations and in your cemeteries and on the departure of them that sleep.[5]

A. The Vigil or Wake

In most places a vigil or wake is held at a funeral home or at the home of the deceased prior to the funeral. Some churches are prepared to have the body brought directly to the church and have the vigil take place there, either in a chapel or in the church itself. Some older city churches contain mortuary chapels intended for laying out the bodies of the faithful departed.

Whether the wake is at the church or at the funeral home, it often includes a period of formal worship led by the parish priest or deacon. If the wake is at the church, the leader may wear cassock and surplice, or alb, and a white stole and, if desired, a cope for a priest or dalmatic for a deacon. At other locations, vestments are not usually worn.

The prayers at the wake may be quite brief, or much fuller. The use of the Litany at the Time of Death (BCP 462-464) or the Prayer for a Vigil (BCP 465-466) is particularly recommended. A Commendatory Prayer (BCP 465) may also be used. If a fuller form of service is desired, a collect, one or two psalms, and a reading from scripture, chosen from those appointed for the burial rite but not being used at the funeral, may precede the litany. It is helpful if the parish (or the undertaker) provides a card with texts to which people are expected to respond during the vigil. If the vigil is at the church, the family may move to a nearby room following the prayers to greet their friends. Refreshments may also be available there.

Bodies, particularly but not exclusively those of the bishop or parish clergy, sometimes lie in state before the altar of the church, with the paschal

---

5. *Didascalia Apostolorum* XXVI, vi, 22, ed. R. Hugh Connolly (Oxford: Clarendon Press, 1929), 252.

candle burning near the coffin, while a prayer vigil is kept. The bodies of clergy are traditionally laid out in the eucharistic vestments proper to their order: alb, stole, and chasuble for priests and bishops, and alb, stole, and dalmatic for deacons. A mitre may be set on top of the pall at a bishop's funeral, and a stole at the funeral of priests and deacons.

If it is desired to have more formal prayers during the vigil, the recommended psalms, readings, and prayers may be used as an office with appropriate canticles.

B. Reception of the Body

When the body is brought to the church, it is met by the priest (or other officiant) at the church door (BCP 466). If the funeral is to follow immediately, all are vested for the funeral. If it is brought to the church before the vigil, a priest vests in alb or surplice and stole and may wear a cope. A deacon vests in alb or surplice and stole and may wear a dalmatic. A lay reader vests in alb or surplice. A member of the congregation carries the lighted paschal candle before the body. If other clergy or servers participate, they walk between the paschal candle and the officiant. The priest may sprinkle the coffin with holy water. The coffin may be covered with the pall, or, if the funeral does not immediately follow, it may be done before the service. The officiant says the bidding and prayers in *The Book of Common Prayer* (BCP 466-467). During the procession the officiant may recite a suitable psalm or anthem, or, if there are singers, one may be sung. The paschal candle is placed in its stand between the body and the altar. The vigil prayers described above may follow.

If the body is brought to the church immediately before the funeral, the opening anthem of the funeral service accompanies the procession.

C. Burial of the Dead: Rite Two

The service is a eucharist or eucharistic Word liturgy. It "should be held at a time when the congregation has opportunity to be present" (BCP 490). In cities this frequently means that funerals are held in the evening, with the committal at the cemetery the following day. Ideally the service should be conducted much like the Sunday parish liturgy, with music, the use of lectors, servers, and assisting clergy. If a choir is not available, the use of a cantor can make the singing of some of the choral elements possible, and instrumental music may be used. The lessons should be chosen by the priest in consultation with the family of the deceased, and together they decide who will read them.

The body is normally placed at the front of the nave with its feet toward the altar. The paschal candle is placed in a stand between the coffin and the altar. It should be placed slightly to the liturgical north side, so that the ministers may stand at the coffin for the commendation. Traditionally the bodies of bishops and priests are placed with their head toward the altar, so that they are facing the congregation. The coffin is covered with a pall when it is brought into the church. The national flag may be substituted for the pall when appropriate.

a. Entrance Rite

The clergy meet the body at the church door, unless it is already in place before the altar. The pall is placed on the coffin. If it is the custom of the parish, the priest may sprinkle the coffin with holy water before it is covered with the pall. The presider says the prayers for the Reception of the Body (BCP 466-467) if they have not already been said. The paschal candle leads the procession down the center aisle of the church. It may be carried by a member of the congregation in ordinary clothes, or by a server or a deacon. If the processional cross and torches are used, the crucifer and torchbearers follow the candle. The choir, servers, and other vested clergy follow. The deacon (unless carrying the paschal candle) walks before the presider carrying the gospel book. The presider immediately precedes the coffin. The family follow it. Pallbearers may carry the coffin to its place and set it on a prepared trestle, or it may be wheeled down the aisle on a "church truck" (a wheeled dolly undertakers use to move coffins within a church) by two pallbearers, while the others walk beside it.

During the procession the anthem "I am the Resurrection" (Hymnal Appendix S 380, S 381) or "In the midst of life we are in death" (Appendix S 382) is sung. This may be sung by the choir or by a cantor. The rubrics permit the use of another suitable hymn, psalm, or anthem. Usually, "I am the Resurrection" is the best choice. If there is no one to sing it, the anthem may be recited by the presider during the procession.

If the body has been cremated and the ashes are present, the presider may meet the ashes at the door and carry them in procession to the place where the body customarily lies. The ashes may be covered with a white chalice veil or other suitable cloth. They may be placed on a small table before the altar. Alternatively, the ashes may be in place before the service.

If the coffin (or urn of ashes) is already in place before the service, the altar party may enter from the sacristy and stand between the coffin and the altar for the anthem. If no body is present, the altar party may enter in the usual way and go to their places during the anthem, the presider going to the chair.

When all are in place and the anthem is finished, the presider may mention the purpose of the service, asking the prayers of the congregation for the deceased and the bereaved (BCP 492). This is also the time to make helpful announcements, such as where to find the service, how communion will be administered, and who may receive, as well as where the committal will be, and where a reception after the service, if there is one, will be held.

b. Ministry of the Word

The presider, facing the people either from the chair or before the altar, says (or sings), "The Lord be with you," extending the hands in the usual manner. After the response, the presider says (or sings), "Let us pray," and, following a pause for silent prayer, one of the burial collects (BCP 493-494). The prayer for the mourners may follow it.

All sit for the readings. One or two lessons may be read before the gospel. They are read by lay persons chosen by the presider and the family, friends of the deceased or the usual parish readers. A psalm, hymn, or canticle may follow each (BCP 494). A special collect and readings for the burial of a child are given (BCP 494, 490). The psalms may be sung or read in any of the ways appropriate for a Sunday liturgy. The gospel is read (or sung) by a deacon (or assisting priest, or the presider, if there is no deacon) with the customary ceremonial. A gospel procession, with lights and incense, is appropriate.

c. The Homily

The prayer book permits a homily, not a eulogy. This does not mean that it is inappropriate to mention significant facts about the person's life as a part of our witness to the power of Christ's resurrection, but the homily should proclaim the gospel. A better time for the sharing of memories about the deceased is at the more informal vigil, rather than during the funeral service. A homily is not required, and was unusual in the Episcopal Church until recently, although they are commonly preached at funerals today. The homily may be given by the presider, "a member of the family, or a friend" (BCP 495). Presumably that includes ministers other than the presider.

The Apostles' Creed may follow the homily, proclaiming "the assurance of eternal life given at Baptism" (BCP 496). Its use is optional, but the rationale given in its introduction is a powerful argument for its use. The presider says the introduction facing the people from the chair, then begins the creed.

d. The Prayers of the People

If the eucharist is not to be celebrated the presider introduces the Lord's Prayer before the prayers of the people (BCP 496), This may take the form, "Let us pray in the words our Savior taught us," or the form introducing that version of the Lord's Prayer at the eucharist. If there is no eucharist one or more of the Additional Prayers (BCP 503-505) given after the committal may be substituted for the prayers of the people.

The eucharistic prayers of the people may be either the form included in Rite Two (BCP 497), the form from Rite One adapted to Rite Two language (BCP 480-481), or the Prayers for a Vigil (BCP 465-466). The prayers are led by a deacon, lay intercessor, or an assisting priest. If a minister of another church is participating in the funeral, it would be appropriate for that minister to lead the prayers. The petition in the Rite Two form referring to baptism is omitted if the deceased is not baptized, and that referring to communion if the deceased is not a communicant. The prayers may be led from the lectern or from the midst of the congregation. The presider concludes the prayers with one of the appointed collects (BCP 498).

If the eucharist is not celebrated, the commendation (BCP 499-500) follows immediately.

e. At the Eucharist

The confession and absolution are omitted, and the liturgy continues with the peace and the offertory. The peace is exchanged in the usual way. It is fitting for friends of the deceased to bring forward the gifts of bread and wine. They are given to a deacon or (if there is no deacon) an assisting priest standing behind the altar, as at other celebrations.

The eucharist is celebrated in the usual manner. If the altar is censed at the offertory, the coffin may also be censed. After censing the gifts, the presider begins at the center of the altar and walks counter-clock wise around the altar swinging the thurible, then goes to the coffin and walks counter-clockwise around the coffin, and returns to complete the circuit of the altar. The people may then be censed by the thurifer.

Any of the appointed eucharistic prayers may be used. The proper preface Of the Commemoration of the Dead is used with prayers A or B, which suggests one of them as choices.

It is most helpful if an usher or server assists members of the congregation unfamiliar with parish custom to come forward at the right time and to the right place to receive communion.

If the text of the proper post-communion prayer (BCP 498) is not printed in the bulletin, the presider must announce the page in the prayer book.

f. The Commendation

Following the post-communion prayer, or the prayers of the people if the eucharist is not celebrated, the presider and other ministers take their place at the body, facing it and the congregation. If the bishop is present, the bishop presides at the commendation. The crucifer and torchbearers stand at the opposite end of the coffin facing it but far enough away to enable the priest to walk around the coffin. If incense and holy water are used, the thurifer and the server carrying the bucket of holy water and the sprinkler stand near the priest. The anthem "Give rest, O Christ" is sung by the choir or cantor (Hymn 355, Appendix S 383). If there is no one to sing it, it may be read by one of the ministers, the congregation joining in the italicized portions. There is a metrical version of the anthem in *The Hymnal 1982* (Hymn 358). The plural forms "servants" and "they" in the first stanza may be altered to the singular.

The presider walks around the coffin counter-clockwise, sprinkling it with holy water and censing it while the anthem is sung or read. If incense and holy water are not used, the presider remains in place during the anthem.

Following the anthem, the presider says or sings the commendatory prayer (BCP 499), facing the body with hands in the orans position. A server may hold the book.

A blessing is permitted, but there seems little reason to follow the commendation with a blessing of those in church, and the service in church appropriately concludes with the dismissal by a deacon or other minister (BCP 500).

g. The Procession from the Church

The presider, other clergy, and servers take their places between the body and the crucifer, while the pallbearers turn the body around. If the paschal candle is to lead the procession from the church, the bearer takes the candle from its stand and moves to a place at the head of the procession. If incense is to be used in the procession, the thurifer follows the paschal candle and precedes the crucifer. The presider walks directly in front of the body, and the family follow it. The singers may remain in their places to sing the anthems or canticles that accompany the procession, or they may take their places behind the crucifer in the procession.

During the procession one or more of the appointed anthems may be sung (BCP 500). Music is in *The Hymnal 1982* (Appendix S 384–S 388, Hymns 354-356). Alternatively, the Song of Zechariah (*Benedictus*), the Song of Simeon (*Nunc dimittis*), Christ our Passover (*Pascha nostrum*), or a hymn may be sung, or instrumental music may be played.

When everyone is in place, the presider turns to face the church door and the procession leaves the church. Where burial is in the churchyard, or ashes are placed in a columbarium in the church, the procession may move directly to the grave and the singing continue until all are in place. The pall is removed from the coffin at the church door.

In most cases the coffin is placed in a hearse and those going to the cemetery accompany it in automobiles. If the cemetery is far away, it may be desirable for the clergy to remove their vestments and either conduct the service at the grave in ordinary clothes or revest upon arrival.

h. The Committal

If the singers have accompanied the procession to the grave, the committal anthem may be sung (BCP 501, Hymnal Appendix S 389). Otherwise, the anthem will be recited by the presider when all are at the grave site. The presider stands at the head of the coffin. If the cross and torchbearers are present, they stand either at the other end of the coffin, or at the side opposite the family facing the grave.

If there are necessary announcements they are made before the service, preferably by the priest. The body is traditionally placed in the grave during the anthem. If the grave has not been blessed, the presider, if a priest, may bless the grave before the committal, using the form in *The Book of Common Prayer* (BCP 503). The sign of the cross may be made at the words "Bless, we pray, this grave," and the grave may be sprinkled with holy water.

The body may be sprinkled with holy water and censed when it is placed in the grave. Unless the burial is in the church or churchyard, incense will probably not be used, although the priest may carry holy water for committals in a small portable sprinkler.

At the conclusion of the anthem, the presider says the sentence of committal (BCP 501) while earth is cast upon the coffin. The priest traditionally casts the first handful or shovelful of earth, and the mourners may continue by adding more earth. Ideally, the family and friends will fill up the grave. In practice this is usually impossible to arrange, and the casting of earth remains symbolic, although it should at least be real earth, not flower petals or sanitized sand.

After the committal, the presider greets the people with "The Lord be with you," and all say the Lord's Prayer together. The presider may then add any appropriate prayers (BCP 503-505). The service concludes with the presider saying, "Rest eternal grant to *him*, O Lord" and the dismissal or the blessing (BCP 502-503).

If the burial is not in the ground, the alterations suggested in the prayer book are made in the sentence of committal, and the casting of earth is omitted.

The committal may be used prior to a cremation, substituting the words "the elements" for "the ground." It may also be used at the interment of ashes, with appropriate changes if necessary.

The committal may, if necessary, take place in the church. If it immediately follows the funeral liturgy, the commendation is omitted and the committal takes its place. In most cases, it seems preferable to use the commendation in church and to have the committal at the place of burial, or, if necessary because of bad weather, in a cemetery chapel. In any case, the actual sentence of committal should be said at the place of burial, even if it is said after most people have left.

D. Burial of the Dead: Rite One

The Rite One funeral service is conducted in the same manner as the Rite Two service described in the previous section, except as noted below.

Some parishioners may wish to be buried with the Rite One liturgy even if that liturgy is not extensively used in the congregation, and clergy need to be sensitive to these requests, especially if they were left as instructions by the deceased.

The prayers for the Reception of the Body may be conformed to Rite One language if they are used at the beginning of the service (BCP 14). There is no rubric permitting greeting and announcements at the beginning of the service, but they are nonetheless appropriate after the opening anthem. Music for the Rite One opening anthem is in the Appendix to *The Hymnal 1982* (S 375–S 378).

The version of the psalms from the 1928 *Book of Common Prayer* and Psalm 23 from the King James Version are included in the Rite One services, presumably because of their familiarity to people who worshiped from the older prayer book for most of their lives. These may be sung or said in the same way as the contemporary versions of the psalms.

No introduction to the Apostles' Creed is included in Rite One, but that from Rite Two can be used, if the creed is to be said.

The form of the prayers of the people on pages 480-481, with the permissible omission of four paragraphs, is used. The deacon (or other leader) leads the prayers, standing at the lectern, or in whatever place the prayers of the people are customarily said.

Either of the two eucharistic prayers for Rite One may be used, with the proper preface of the Commemoration of the Dead. The proper post-communion prayer (BCP 482) replaces the usual prayer.

There are two alternative anthems for the committal. Music for the first and second are in the Appendix to *The Hymnal 1982* (S 379 and S389).

E. Funerals Without the Eucharist

A priest or deacon presiding normally wears alb or cassock and surplice and white stole. A priest may also wear a cope and a deacon a dalmatic. The paschal candle is carried before the body, and all the ceremonial described for the eucharist may be followed. All is done as above, except that only one scripture reading is required, and that need not be the gospel. It is, of course, proper to use the full number of readings and psalms, unless it is desirable to shorten the service further.

The presider introduces the Lord's Prayer immediately before the prayers of the people. The prayers of the people may be said in the usual way, as above, or various prayers from the selection of additional prayers may be used in their place. This may be helpful if there is no one but the presider to lead the prayers and the congregation is unfamiliar with the traditional forms. In most cases, it is best to use one of the forms authorized for Rite Two burial as above (BCP 496).

The commendation follows the prayers of the people, and all else is done as described above.

F. Funerals Without a Priest

If no priest or bishop is available, a deacon or lay reader may preside. The directions for funerals without a eucharist are followed. A deacon wears cassock, surplice, and white stole, or an alb and stole, and may also wear a dalmatic over the alb. A lay reader wears either cassock and surplice, or alb, according to parish custom. It is permissible, if it is the local custom, for the presider to cense the coffin and sprinkle it with holy water. If there is no deacon to read the gospel, a lector or the presider may read it as a lesson.

Except for the consecration of the grave, a deacon or lay reader may preside at the committal in the absence of a priest.

G. An Order for Burial

This order is intended for use "when, for pastoral considerations, neither of the burial rites in [*The Book of Common Prayer*] is deemed appropriate" (BCP 506). Possible uses include a church funeral in which prayers from earlier prayer books are substituted for those in the present rites, a funeral at which non-prayer book material is used, or a funeral conducted for a congregation unfamiliar with Episcopal liturgy.

The body may be set in place before the congregation assembles, or the presider may meet the body at the church door and conduct it into the church. This may be done as described above, or the presider may simply walk before the body into the church.

Any of the anthems from the burial service, any of the proper psalms, or a hymn may accompany this procession.

"Prayer may be offered for the bereaved" (BCP 506). This may be a collect from the burial service or another suitable prayer.

One or more readings from scripture follow. A psalm, hymn, or anthem may follow each reading. If the eucharist is celebrated, the final reading is from the gospel. This may, of course, be done exactly as in the description above, but more flexibility in the readings is allowed. A homily may follow the last reading, and the Apostles' Creed may be said.

"Prayer, including the Lord's Prayer, is offered for the deceased, for those who mourn, and for the Christian community, remembering the promises of God in Christ about eternal life" (BCP 506). This gives the presider almost complete freedom to choose any suitable prayers, including those in the Rite One and Rite Two burial services.

If the eucharist is celebrated, the peace is exchanged and the bread and wine brought forward to the altar. "Any of the authorized eucharistic prayers may be used" (BCP 506).

The deceased is commended to God in some appropriate way, and the body is committed to its resting place. This is exactly what the regular burial rites do, but in this case, no specific forms are required.

Although, like the other burial rites, this order assumes that the funeral will take place in a church or chapel, it provides what may be a useful set of variations for a funeral conducted in the home of the deceased or in a funeral home.

H. Burial of One Who Does Not Profess the Christian Faith

The Book of Occasional Services contains forms to be used with An Order for Burial for the funeral of a non-Christian (BOS 175-178). The most frequent use of this form is for the funeral of a non-Christian member of a Christian family. An alternative opening anthem, alternative lessons, psalms, prayers, and a committal are included. The second prayer under For the Deceased is an alternative to the commendatory prayer (BOS 176). Such a service may appropriately be conducted in a funeral home, but it may also be held in the church, if that is the family's wish.

At the committal, the form in *The Book of Occasional Services* (BOS 178) replaces that in the prayer book. The commendatory prayer (BOS 176) and other appropriate prayers may follow the committal.

I. Funerals in Houses or Funeral Homes

It is the expectation of the Episcopal Church that the funerals of Christians will be held in the church. There are, nevertheless, many occasions on which Episcopal clergy are asked to conduct funerals in funeral homes, or in private houses. Normally, such funerals do not include the eucharist. If the eucharist is to be celebrated in connection with a funeral not in the church, it is usually held at another time for the family or for the members of the congregation.

Some clergy vest in cassock, surplice, and white stole for funerals outside the church. Others wear clerical street dress. A lay reader should conduct such a service only under the direction of the pastor of the congregation. A lay reader may wear cassock and surplice. As at all other funerals, the coffin is closed before the service.

The service may follow the Rite One or Rite Two form, with necessary ceremonial modifications. Booklets containing at least the congregation's parts of the service must be distributed. Such booklets will often be provided by the funeral director, if arrangements are made well beforehand. If it is not possible for the congregation to make the responses, it may be desirable to follow An Order for Burial (BCP 506-507).

The officiant enters and stands near the coffin. Frequently a lectern is provided. The officiant reads the opening anthem, makes any appropriate announcements about the service, and continues the service with the salutation and collect(s).

Lay persons may read the scripture lessons, or the officiant does so. Unless the people have the words of the psalms, they will have to be read by an individual or sung as a solo. If the officiant does not read the lessons, the reader comes to the lectern and the officiant sits in a convenient chair. If there is a gospel reading, it is last, and the officiant reads it unless there are other clergy participating. The officiant, or some other person, may give a homily after the last reading.

If the person was baptized, the officiant may lead the congregation in the Apostles' Creed. This may be introduced as in Rite Two (BCP 496).

The officiant invites the people to join in the Lord's Prayer. Other prayers may either precede or follow it, but it should either be first or last.

The officiant stands in front of the coffin and says the anthem for the commendation and the commendatory prayer. If the deceased is not a Christian, the form "Into your hands, O God" from *The Book of Occasional Services* (BOS 176) is used.

The committal is conducted in the usual manner. If the person is not a Christian the alternative committal from *The Book of Occasional Services* (BOS 178) is used.

J. Funerals Without a Body or Ashes

A funeral service may be held without the presence of the body or cremated remains if the body is unavailable, or has already been buried. The service is conducted as above. The procession enters in the usual manner and the presider goes to the chair. The opening anthem is sung during the entry or, if necessary, recited when all are in place.

The commendation is omitted (BCP 482, 499) and the service concludes with (the blessing and) dismissal.

K. Memorial Services

These are services held on anniversaries of a death, or in places other than where the funeral is celebrated. They also include celebrations such as Memorial Day and All Souls' Day, or similar local celebrations on which the eucharist is offered for the faithful departed.

These services are normally celebrations of the eucharist with the propers For the Departed from Various Occasions in *The Book of Common Prayer* (BCP 928). A rubric permits the use of any of the collects from the Burial of the Dead as alternatives. Collects and lessons for All Faithful Departed (November 2), commonly called All Souls' Day, are in *Lesser Feasts and Fasts*.

Unlike a funeral, a memorial service begins with the opening acclamation and the usual eucharistic entrance rite. Since the liturgy of the dead is an Easter liturgy, the use of the Easter acclamation, "Alleluia. Christ is risen," is appropriate. The use of the *Kyrie eleison* or *Trisagion* will probably be most suitable.

For the prayers of the people, any of the usual forms, or those appointed for a burial, may be used. The proper preface is that of the Commemoration of the Dead. One of the usual post-communion prayers, or one in the funeral liturgy, may be used.

If the memorial service is not a eucharist, it may be in the form of a Liturgy of the Word. If an office of the dead is desired for a memorial service, either Morning or Evening Prayer (depending on the time of day) may be used with psalms and readings chosen from those for the funeral liturgy.

Chapter Four

Episcopal Services

The role of the bishop in many of services of the church has already been discussed in some detail elsewhere: Howard Galley's *The Ceremonies of the Eucharist*, for example, contains chapters on The Bishop at Parish Eucharists, The Bishop at Holy Baptism, and The Ordination of Priests and Deacons. The first of these chapters also contains general information about the role of the bishop in the liturgy and the use of deacons and lay assistants to assist the bishop. Some directions for the bishop are also included in *Lent, Holy Week, Easter, and the Great Fifty Days,* and in the descriptions of particular services in this book.

In general, the bishop presides at services when present. The bishop may always preside in the same manner as a priest, using neither mitre nor pastoral staff, or the bishop may use them only at the entrance and exit processions and while giving the final blessing.

A section in chapter twelve of Galley's book discusses the bishop's role at celebrations by a presbyter. If participating in other rites without presiding, the bishop generally pronounces absolutions and blessing. At a marriage, for example, "when both a bishop and a priest are present and officiating, the bishop should pronounce the blessing and preside at the Eucharist" (BCP 422). At a funeral, the bishop presides at the eucharist and pronounces the commendation (BCP 468, 490). Sufficient indications of the role of the bishop are given when the various services are discussed so as not to require further treatment.

Although Anglicans tend to picture their bishops in cope and mitre, the bishop properly wears chasuble and mitre when presiding at the eucharist and rites attached to it. For non-eucharistic services the bishop may wear alb (or rochet) and cope and mitre, or choir dress (rochet and chimere). For simple services the bishop may wear an alb or rochet (without the chimere) and stole. The bishop wears a stole at services for which the presider normally does so: a bishop's stole, or pallium, may be worn over the chasuble, although this use is not common, or the bishop may wear the same stole as a priest. The stole is not properly worn over a chimere. The rochet and chimere are a bishop's choir vestments, and unless the stole is white the colors will clash with a scarlet chimere. The bishop wears choir dress when participating in the daily offices, but wears cope and mitre and may carry the staff to preside at Solemn Evensong, or other solemn offices. The bishop wears the pectoral cross over the alb or rochet and under a cope or chasuble, although increasingly bishops wear the cross over the chasuble, especially if the chasuble is not highly ornamented.

The bishop's mitre is worn when entering and leaving the church in procession, and during other formal processions such as the Palm Sunday or Candlemas processions, the processions at the Easter Vigil, and those to the baptistry. The bishop also may wear the mitre when seated. It is not worn during prayers (other than the litany in procession), during the gospel, and from the beginning of the eucharistic prayer through the post-communion prayer.

There is a diversity in the use of the pastoral staff in the Anglican Communion. Some understand the staff to be a part of the bishop's insignia, presented at ordination and used by all bishops, while others see it as signifying jurisdiction and restrict its use to the diocesan bishop. Some diocesan bishops have given staves to their suffragans. In general, the staff is used only by diocesan bishops. Other bishops use it at the pleasure of the diocesan, usually only when representing the diocesan.

The pastoral staff is carried by the bishop in the left hand with the crook outward. When it is not being carried by the bishop it is held by a server or placed in a stand.

In practice, it is often difficult to follow these rules, especially in small churches in which there is neither the space nor the people available for the bishop to have mitre and staff bearers, as well as two deacons. A stand for the pastoral staff placed near enough to the bishop's chair that, if necessary, the bishop may put the staff in it without the assistance of deacons or servers is often useful. It is also helpful to have a small table available where the mitre can be placed when not being worn.

Even so, bishops often find themselves standing at fonts or in the center of the sanctuary wearing the mitre with no convenient place to put it, and so they wear it during the prayers. This is certainly preferable to making a major issue over where to put the mitre. If it is necessary to place the mitre on the altar, it should be laid flat so it is not conspicuous, rather than stood upright. It is not reasonable to expect an acolyte to hold a mitre in ungloved hands throughout large parts of the service. The traditional solution is for the mitre bearer to wear a *vimpa*, a silk scarf through which to hold the mitre, but this seems incredibly fussy to most people today.

The question has been raised of whether it might not be better for the bishop to wear the mitre during the prayer of consecration at ordinations, the thanksgiving over the water and chrism at baptism, and similar prayers, since these are official episcopal acts, and the mitre is the visible symbol of the bishop's office. This is certainly a reasonable, if untraditional, rationale for doing something that is convenient, if not actually necessary, and deserves serious consideration.

1. The Bishop in the Parish Liturgy

It is the bishop's prerogative, when present, to be the principal celebrant at the Lord's Table, and to preach the Gospel. (BCP 322, 354)

The bishop, when present, is the celebrant; and is expected to preach the Word and preside at Baptism and the Eucharist. (BCP 298)

It is appropriate that the other priests present stand with the celebrant at the Altar, and join in the consecration of the gifts, in breaking the Bread, and in distributing Communion. (BCP 322, 354)

These three rubrics from *The Book of Common Prayer* set the liturgical parameters of the bishop's visitation. The bishop presides at the eucharist and preaches the gospel. Normally the clergy of the parish stand with the bishop at the altar as concelebrants. The bishop will also ideally preside at baptism, consecrate chrism, and confirm in this context. Details of these rites are given in chapter fourteen of *Ceremonies of the Eucharist* and in the section on Rites Related to Christian Initiation above.

The bishop may also participate in marriage and funeral liturgies in the parish, as described in the sections of this book concerned with those rites.

The ordination of priests and deacons also frequently takes place in parish churches. These rites are described by Galley in chapter fifteen.

The bishop's *cathedra* is in the cathedral. Since the late nineteenth century many churches have had bishop's chairs decorated with mitres and usually sitting empty on the liturgical north side of the sanctuary. There is certainly no reason why the bishop should not use such chairs where they exist, but in parish churches the bishop normally presides from the presider's chair used by priests.

2. Celebration of a New Ministry

"This order," according to *The Book of Common Prayer*, "is for use when a priest is being instituted and inducted as rector of a parish" (BCP 558). It replaces An Office of Institution of Ministers in the 1928 prayer book and may be adapted for the beginning of other ministries. In practice it is used with great flexibility, and the freedom given in planning specific services is not always wisely used. There is considerable sentiment for the revision or replacement of the service in the next revision of the prayer book.

A. For Instituting a Rector

As the service is set forth in the prayer book, the bishop presides. Other priests of the congregation "stand with the chief celebrant at the Altar," and parish deacons "assist according to their order" (BCP 558). Ministers of other churches are appropriately included in the service. If the bishop is represented by a deputy, the priest being instituted presides at the eucharist (BCP 558).

A chair for the institutor is placed at the entrance of the chancel, of the sanctuary, "or in some other place where the bishop and other ministers may be clearly seen and heard by the people" (BCP 564). The exact placement will depend on the arrangement of the church. The symbols to be presented to the new rector may be placed on a table at the side of the church, or some other convenient location, until they are needed.

The details of the service, including order of entrance procession, manner of receiving communion, and the nature and number of the symbols to be presented need to be carefully worked out ahead of time, and a program prepared for the service.

The bishop vests for the eucharist, wearing the mitre and carrying the staff. The priest being instituted wears an alb, and puts on the stole (and chasuble) after receiving them in the course of the service.[1] If only the stole is being presented, the chasuble may be laid out on the altar rail for the priest to put on with the stole. Unless the priest is to preside at the eucharist, the chasuble may be omitted and the concelebrants wear alb and stole. Those parish priests who will concelebrate wear alb and stole. If they are to wear chasubles, they may wear them from the beginning of the service or put them on when the new rector does. The deacons vest in alb, stole, and dalmatic.

The procession enters the church during a hymn, psalm, or anthem. If incense is used, it is blessed by the bishop before the procession begins. The thurifer leads the procession, followed by crucifer and torchbearers, the choir, servers, clergy of other churches, diocesan clergy, parish clergy, the new rector escorted by the churchwardens, and the bishop. A parish deacon may walk in front of the new rector carrying the gospel book. If there is no parish deacon another deacon may do this. Two other deacons (or priests, if there are not sufficient deacons) may walk on either side of the bishop. Two servers are designated to hold the bishop's mitre and staff when they are not in use. They should have places near the bishop in the sanctuary, and if there are no deacons or priests walking with the bishop in the procession, they may do so.

The bishop goes directly to the chair in the middle of the chancel (or sanctuary). The priest being instituted stands before the bishop with the wardens on each side. The churchwardens present the new rector to the bishop (BCP 559), and there may be additional presenters (BCP 565). The bishop then reads the letter of institution (BCP 557) or states the nature of the new ministry.

---

1. Bishop Marshall recommends that the rector enter wearing stole and chasuble to avoid the suggestion that this is an ordination, at which the changing of vesture signifies the entry into a new order of ministry.

The bishop then asks the new minister and the congregation the questions from *The Book of Common Prayer* (BCP 559). The bishop stands, removes the mitre and hands it to the server, and asks the congregation's prayers for the new rector.

The Litany for Ordinations follows. It may be sung or said. Although the litanist is often a priest, there is no reason why a precentor from the choir should not lead the litany. All may stand or kneel. In either case, at the end of the litany the bishop stands to sing (or say), "The Lord be with you," and the appointed collect.

The collect and any of the readings may be those of the day, rather than those appointed. The collect and readings of the day should certainly be used on principal feasts. On Sundays in Advent, Lent, and Easter preference should be given to the propers of the day. On other Sundays the readings may be selected from among the various choices. On weekdays the propers for the new ministry are appropriate.

The lessons before the gospel are read by lay members of the congregation. The bishop sits and puts on the mitre. The presenters go to their seats. The new rector goes to a seat at the front of the congregation. The psalms are sung (or said) in the manner customary at parish Sunday liturgies. A deacon (or an assisting priest, if no deacon is present) reads the gospel, with the customary procession and ceremonial. The deacon may come to the bishop for a blessing before reading the gospel. During the gospel the bishop stands without the mitre, holding the staff.

> The sermon may be preached by the bishop, the new minister, or some other person; or an address about the work of the congregation and of the new minister may be made. Representatives of the congregation or of the community, the bishop, or other persons present, may speak in response to the address or sermon. (BCP 565)

It is the bishop's prerogative to preach or to designate the preacher. If the new rector does not preach, he or she may speak in response to the sermon. The responses should be brief, so as not to prolong the service unduly.

A congregational hymn follows the sermon and responses (BCP 560). The new rector comes forward and stands at the entrance to the chancel (or sanctuary). Representatives of the congregation and clergy come forward one after another to present the various symbols. Additional symbols may be added, but it is important that the entire process be taken seriously. At a reception in the parish house, *not* during the service, is the time to make humorous or lighthearted presentations. Those during the service should reflect the nature of the ministry being inaugurated. The bishop concludes the presentations, saying, "*N.*, let all these be signs of the ministry which is mine and yours in this place" (BCP 562).

The new rector then kneels in the midst of the church facing the altar and says the prayer, "O Lord my God, I am not worthy." The bishop then presents the new rector to the congregation (BCP 563). The rector's family may also be presented at this time. The people applaud.

The bishop greets the new rector with the peace, and the new rector faces the people and says, "The peace of the Lord be always with you." The exchange of the peace follows, with the new rector greeting the other clergy, family, friends, and congregation. This may take some time.

The priest vests in the stole (and chasuble) presented. If no chasuble is presented, the rector may concelebrate in alb and stole, or chasubles may be laid out for the parish priests who will concelebrate to put on at this time.

The bishop says the offertory sentence. A deacon goes to the altar. The bread and wine presented to the rector earlier and as much additional bread and wine as is needed are brought to the deacon. A server brings the vessels to the altar. The rector brings forward the bread and wine already presented and representatives of the congregation bring up the additional bread and wine. The deacon prepares the table.

The bishop goes to the altar. A deacon stands at the bishop's right, the new rector at the left, and the other concelebrating priests on either side. Only the other priests who serve in the congregation stand at the altar with the bishop and new rector. Other priests present remain in the choir or nave.

Any of the authorized eucharistic prayers may be used (BCP 565). Except on major feasts, the preface for Apostles and Ordinations may be used. Note, however, that some eucharistic prayers do not permit the use of a proper preface. The bishop, the new rector, and other designated ministers communicate the congregation.

A proper post-communion prayer replaces the usual prayer (BCP 564). The bishop may, and usually does, ask the new rector to pronounce the blessing.

B. A Deputy as Institutor

If the bishop is not the institutor, the deputy presides at the service until the offertory. When the vessel of water is presented at the induction, the deputy follows the altered text (BCP 561). After the new rector has greeted the people, he or she becomes the presider and chief celebrant at the eucharist. The deputy may stand at the altar with the new rector and other priests of the parish as a concelebrant. The institutor leads the congregation in the proper post-communion prayer.

The deputy, if a concelebrant, wears eucharistic vestments. Otherwise alb, stole, and cope may be worn.

C. The Inauguration of Other Ministries

This order... may also be used for the installation of deans and canons of cathedrals, or the inauguration of other ministries, diocesan or parochial, including vicars of missions and assistant ministers. Alterations in the service are then made according to circumstances. (BCP 558)

When the order is used for the installation of other clergy who have pastoral and sacramental ministries, such as cathedral deans and canons, or vicars, few changes are necessary beyond the title of the office. In particular cases presentations of other symbols are appropriate.

Cathedral deans and canons may be "installed," that is, led to their stalls in choir and formally seated. In the case of canons this is done by the dean. For the dean, this may be done by the bishop and a representative of the cathedral chapter. It should follow the prayer said kneeling by the person being installed, and precede his or her presentation to the congregation.

In the case of the installation of ministers such as diocesan canons, whose ministry may not include sacramental and pastoral ministry to the congregation, greater adaptation will be needed. Some of the presentations can be omitted or rewritten to describe the ministry properly.

For the ministry of assistants, deacons, and lay ministers, for whom the letter of institution is not appropriate, a description of the ministry "and the authority being conferred" is given by the institutor (BCP 565). This may or may not be in the form of a written document signed by the bishop.

For the new ministry of an assistant priest, the presider will normally be the rector, although the bishop or other diocesan representative may preside instead.

For the ministry of a parish deacon, the service will require more extensive adaptation. The North American Association for the Diaconate has resources available that make appropriate alterations for a deacon. During the service,

> the new minister, if a deacon, should read the Gospel, prepare the elements at the Offertory, assist the celebrant at the Altar, and dismiss the congregation. (BCP 558)

In order to do this effectively the presentation of symbols should follow the litany. The presider presents the deacon with the book of gospels as the principal symbol of diaconal ministry, using words such as, "N., be among us as a herald of God's words and deeds."[2] Other appropriate symbols may then be presented, including the deacon's stole and dalmatic. The deacon reads the gospel and is presented to the congregation. At the offertory, the deacon goes to the altar, receives the gifts of the people, and prepares the table for the eucharist. The deacon stands at the presider's right during the Great Thanksgiving, performing the customary diaconal role. The deacon joins in ministering communion. At the conclusion of the liturgy, the deacon dismisses the people.

If the new ministry of a lay person is being celebrated, the presentations may also take place at the conclusion of the litany, so that the lay person may read one of the lessons. The presentations need to be appropriate to the ministry involved. The lay minister assists in whatever is appropriate to that ministry. The proper post-communion prayer is not used. Note that for most lay ministries the form Commissioning for Lay Ministries in the Church described above from *The Book of Occasional Services* is the appropriate service inaugurating their ministry.

---

2. Edwin F. Hallenbeck, *A Working Paper of Trial Liturgy for Celebration of Deacon's Ministry* (Providence, R. I.: North American Association for the Diaconate, 1996), 3.

D. Installation of Ministry Teams

In some places, such as the Diocese of Northern Michigan, the service has been adapted for the installation of a team of ordained and lay ministers, so that the entire installation is set in the context of the renewal of baptismal vows by the congregation. Such creative uses of the rite are to be encouraged, but it is impossible to discuss their details in general. Each one is crafted for a particular situation, and some are replacements of the prayer book order rather than adaptations of it.

3. Consecration of Churches

The Dedication and Consecration of a Church is intended for use at the opening of a church or chapel. Apparently in conflict with Title II, Canon 7, the service "does not require that the premises be debt-free or owned" (BCP 575). A special order for the consecration of a church "long in use" is also given (BCP 577).

Many congregations will never use this service, and few will use it more than once. It requires a great deal of advance planning and preparation, since, as the prayer book notes, "it is desirable that all members of the congregation, young and old, have some individual or collective part in the celebration, as well as the architect, builders, musicians, artists, benefactors, and friends" (BCP 566). The use of a printed program containing the service is almost a necessity.

The bishop presides. If the service is conducted on a Sunday, a major feast, or the patronal feast of the church, selections from the proper of the day may be included; otherwise, the propers are those indicated in the consecration service. The liturgical color is white, unless red is used for a major or patronal feast.

A. Consecration of a New Church

The plan of the service is that the bishop and congregation enter the new building and take possession of it, consecrating the building and its furnishings as they are used. The eucharist and, if possible, baptism form a part of the consecration, and other pastoral offices may be celebrated.

The items to be used in the worship of the new church are carried into the church in the opening procession as far as is practical. Things that cannot be conveniently carried in are placed near where they will be needed. Items that might be carried include a ewer of water for the font, containers of olive oil and aromatic oil called oil of balsam (if the bishop is to consecrate chrism), a Bible or lectionary text for the lectern, the gospel book, the chalice and paten, the altar book, and the eucharistic gifts of bread and wine. These may be carried by their donors or by those who will use them. Things such as altar frontals, candlesticks, and flowers may be carried in procession or brought from the sacristy or a table in the church at the appropriate time. The prayer book also notes that "such things as the deed for the property and the blueprint of the building(s), the keys, and tools used in its construction may also be carried by appropriate persons" (BCP 575). It will be helpful in preparation if lists of the items needed at each place—font, pulpit, lectern, altar, credence table, and so on—are prepared, and those to be carried in procession noted, so that everything may be ready when needed.

a. Entrance Procession

The bishop, clergy, and congregation gather outside the church, either out of doors, in the parish house, or in some other convenient place. If the place where they have formerly worshiped is nearby, they may assemble there and go in procession to the new church. The bishop is vested in alb (or rochet), stole, cope, and mitre, and carries the pastoral staff. The priests of the parish who will stand at the altar with the bishop during the eucharist wear alb and stole, the parish deacons wear alb, stole, and dalmatic, and other clergy wear choir dress. The rector may also wear a cope. The items to be carried in procession are ready at hand. Ushers give everyone programs containing the text of the service and (at least) the music to be sung during the procession.

The bishop gives the opening address to the congregation (BCP 567), removes the mitre, hands the staff to a deacon or chaplain, and says the opening collect with hands in the orans position. The rector may then make any necessary announcements. The bishop resumes the mitre and takes the pastoral staff.

The procession to the church follows this order:

(Thurifer)

Torch   Crucifer   Torch

Choir

Congregation

People Carrying Items

Visiting Clergy

Servers

Parish Deacon(s)

Assisting Priests

Rector

(Deacon or chaplain)   Bishop   (Deacon or chaplain)

Members of the congregation unable to walk in the procession may await it in the church. "When convenient, the procession may go around the building(s) to be dedicated and then go to the principal door" (BCP 575). The bishop may sprinkle the walls of the church with holy water. In case of necessity the congregation may assemble in the church, but the bishop, clergy, and attendants enter in procession through the principal door.

Portable instruments may be used during the procession, but the organ should remain silent until it is dedicated. It is helpful if the music used during the procession is well known to the congregation, so that all may participate.

At the door, the bishop says, "Let the door(s) be opened." The bishop traditionally knocks on the church door with the pastoral staff. A churchwarden or member of the vestry or building committee opens the door from inside. The bishop marks the threshold with a cross, using the pastoral staff, saying "Peace be to his house. . . ." If the bishop does not carry a staff, the foot of the processional cross may be used. The cross on the threshold may be incised, painted, or inlaid. In this case the bishop follows its outline with the staff. The procession enters the church, and choir and congregation go to their places. Psalm 122, or other psalms, hymns, or anthems may be sung (BCP 568).

b. Prayer of Consecration

The bishop goes to the place where the Prayer of Consecration will be said. In most places this will be at the front of the nave, but it may be said from a place near the entrance or in the midst of the church. It should be a place from which the bishop can be seen and heard. The bishop removes the mitre, hands the staff to an attendant, and says the first paragraph of the prayer. The warden, standing beside the bishop, says the second paragraph, and the rector, standing at the other side of the bishop, says the final paragraph. The bishop says the final doxology and the people respond (BCP 569).

c. Blessing of the Font (and Baptism)

The procession now moves to the font. The bishop places a hand on the font and says the prayer of dedication, making the sign of the cross at "We dedicate this font." If possible, baptisms follow. The baptismal gospel is read by a deacon, and the service begins with the presentation of the candidates and concludes with the reception of the newly baptized (BCP 575). The consecration service recommends that children of the congregation pour the water into the font. The bishop appropriately consecrates chrism at this time, as indicated in the baptismal rite.

If there are no baptisms, water is poured into the font and the bishop blesses the water with the form in the consecration service (BCP 570). The bishop may follow the blessing of the water with the consecration of chrism as in the baptismal rite (BCP 575). The bishop may sprinkle the congregation with the baptismal water. The congregation may renew their baptismal vows (BCP 292-294).

d. Dedication of Lectern and Pulpit

The procession moves to the lectern and pulpit, and the bishop dedicates them. Selected psalm or hymn verses may accompany the procession as it moves from place to place. The bishop lays a hand on the lectern (or pulpit) and says the appointed prayer. The versicle may be said by the bishop and the response made by all, or the versicle may be sung by a cantor and the response similarly sung. The bishop says, "We dedicate this...," making the sign of the cross at the invocation of the Trinity. If lectern and pulpit are separate, the lectern is dedicated first. Then the procession moves to the pulpit. If it is desired, the bishop may sprinkle the objects dedicated with water from the font. "As the furnishings in the church are dedicated, they may be decorated by members of the congregation with flowers, candles, hangings, or other ornaments" (BCP 576).

e. Liturgy of the Word

The liturgy then continues with the readings. The Bible or lectionary is brought to the lectern by the reader of the first reading. All sit. The bishop may wear the mitre. All sit for the reading. The psalm following may be said or sung in any of the customary ways. A second lay person reads the epistle.

f. Dedication of the Organ

If the organ (or some other instrument) is to be dedicated, the bishop goes to the appropriate place and dedicates the instrument in the same way as the font and the pulpit. "Instrumental music is now played, or a hymn or anthem sung" (BCP 572). This is the introduction of the organ into the service, and the choice of music should reflect this appropriately.

g. Gospel and Sermon

A deacon (or if there is no deacon, an assisting priest) proclaims the gospel. This should be done in the most solemn manner used in the congregation, with a gospel procession, processional torches, and the use of incense (if that is customary). The bishop stands facing the book, without the mitre, but holding the pastoral staff during the gospel.

The sermon follows. The bishop preaches or designates someone else to do so.

> If there is an address instead of a sermon, it is suitable that a warden or other lay person outline the plans of the congregation for witness to the Gospel. The bishop may respond, indicating the place of this congregation within the life of the Diocese. (BCP 576)

h. Other Pastoral Offices

If other pastoral offices are to be celebrated, they follow the sermon. These might include Thanksgiving for the Birth or Adoption of a Child, Commitment to Christian Service, or Blessing of Oil for the Sick (BCP 576).

If the Apostles' Creed has not already been said in the baptismal context, the Nicene Creed is said or sung.

i. Prayers of the People

The prayers of the people are led by a deacon or a member of the congregation in the customary manner. They may be specially composed for the occasion or one of the usual forms. The bishop recites two fixed prayers at their conclusion (BCP 572-573).

j. Consecration of the Altar

The bishop introduces the consecration of the altar by saying, "Let us now pray for the setting apart of the Altar" (BCP 573). The bishop stands at the center of the altar, with the deacons or chaplains on either side, and says the prayer with arms extended over the altar. All make the response, "Blessed be your Name, Lord God" (BCP 573).

The bishop lays a hand upon the table of the altar and continues the prayer. The bishop may make the sign of the cross on the altar at "sanctify this Table dedicated to you" (BCP 574). If the altar table is stone with crosses marked in it, the bishop traces the incised cross at the center. If there are crosses at the corners of the altar as well, the bishop may also trace those crosses. Following an ancient tradition, the bishop may mark the crosses first with the baptismal water and then with chrism, but this is not required or even suggested by the prayer book.

At the conclusion of the prayer, bells may be rung and music played. Members of the congregation may vest and adorn the altar, and light the altar candles. "It is suitable that the donors of these furnishings, or other lay persons, bring them forward and put them in place" (BCP 574, 576). The vessels are brought forward and placed upon the altar, and the deacon prepares the altar for the eucharist. If incense is used, it is appropriate at this time (BCP 576).

k. The Eucharist

The bishop is the chief celebrant, and the priests of the parish stand at the altar as concelebrants. The bishop may remove the cope and vest in the chasuble before going to the altar. The concelebrating priests may also wear chasubles. If the bishop does not preside, the rector may be designated to do so. The eucharist is celebrated in the usual manner. The proper preface for the Dedication of a Church, or that of the season, or one appropriate to the name of the church is used (BCP 574, 576).

After the post-communion prayer, the bishop blesses the people. The longer form of blessing in the ordination of bishops may appropriately be used (BCP 523). The deacon dismisses the people, and the procession departs.

B. For a Church or Chapel Long in Use

Many church buildings have never been consecrated. For a building that has been used for public worship for "an extended period of time without having been consecrated," an alternative order is given in *The Book of Common Prayer* (BCP 577-579).

The procession takes place as described above, including the entrance into the church and the signing of the threshold by the bishop. At the entrance to the church a Litany of Thanksgiving for a Church (BCP 578-579) is sung. The music is in the Appendix to *The Hymnal 1982* at S 391. The petitions may be sung by the bishop, one of the clergy, or a lay cantor. The *Te Deum* follows the litany. It is sung by the choir and congregation to an appropriate setting. The liturgy of the Word, with a sermon or address, follows.

After the sermon, the bishop leads the congregation in the renewal of baptismal vows. The prayers of the people include intercessions commemorating benefactors of the congregation. The peace is exchanged, and the eucharist is celebrated, beginning with the offertory.

The celebration of baptism and other pastoral offices is suitable in this context, as is the dedication of any new church furnishings.

C. The Dedication of Church Furnishings

The dedication of new furnishings or additions to a church may be celebrated by excerpting the appropriate parts of the service for the consecration of the church. The bishop or a priest uses the appropriate prayers and the new furnishings are put into use.

A new font or baptistry is blessed by a bishop (BCP 577) and, if possible, followed by the celebration of baptism. The blessing of an altar is reserved to bishops, and is always followed by the celebration of the eucharist.

4. Ordination Rites

The ordination rites of the 1979 *Book of Common Prayer* make some different basic assumptions from Cranmer's ordinal of 1550, a revised form of which was in the 1928 prayer book. Thomas Cranmer assumed that ordinations were diocesan services normally to be held in cathedrals. The archdeacon presented a class of diocesan candidates to be ordained deacon and a class of deacons to be ordained priest, and the diocesan bishop ordained them. In a similar way the English archbishops ordained groups, usually small groups, of presbyters to be bishops in the province. Ordinations were seen as basically clerical events, of concern primarily to other clergy. There was no obvious connection between the laity of the parishes from which the ordinands came or to which they were sent and those ordained.

In Cranmer's ordinal the "public prayer" was separated from the laying on of hands, as it was in the Roman and Sarum pontificals, although these two elements were believed to be the essence of ordination. The imposition of hands was accompanied by an imperative formula based on scripture to avoid a "dumb ceremony," such as the Roman tradition of laying on hands in silence. It was a Reformation principle that ceremonies needed to be explained.

The *Book of Common Prayer* attempts to remedy these defects. Most significantly, the laying on of hands is joined to a substantive ordination prayer, and that act for all three orders is called "consecration," the term "ordination" being used for the entire rite for all three orders. This unites the two central elements of ordination.

The prayer book also expects that candidates will be ordained individually, although it does not actually require it. The normative expectation is that deacons and priests will be ordained in the churches in which they will serve. The candidates are presented by clergy and lay people. This clearly establishes the relationship between ordinands and congregations, but it may also have the undesirable effect of making ordination seem more important than baptism.

A. The Ordination of Priests and Deacons

The ordination of priests and deacons, which frequently takes place in parish churches, is described by Howard Galley in *The Ceremonies of the Eucharist*. Each of these services needs to be thoroughly planned and rehearsed and a program provided for the assistance of the congregation. The liturgical color is white or red. If the ordination is on a Sunday or major feast, the color of the day may be used and one or more of the readings and the collect. Frequently there is a diocesan customary for ordinations that normally ought to be followed. Where such a customary exists, the bishop should be asked to approve beforehand any changes from it.

B. The Ordination of Bishops

The Presiding Bishop, or a bishop appointed by the Presiding Bishop, presides. The service is planned in consultation with the Presiding Bishop's office. The assistance both of those experienced in planning such events and those familiar with the requirements of the particular space in which it will be held are important. Normally there will be a large number of participants. The use of space and the roles assigned to the various individuals and groups participating need to be well thought out and planned for. The arrangement of space is particularly important if the service is conducted in an auditorium or civic center. Furthermore, "in accordance with ancient custom, it is desirable, if possible, that bishops be ordained on Sundays and other feasts of our Lord or on the feasts of apostles or evangelists" (BCP 511).

The chair for the Presiding Bishop is placed in the middle of the chancel or sanctuary in front of the altar. The co-consecrators (or at least two of them) sit to the left and right. Other participating bishops may be seated in a line or semicircle on either side of them, or they may be seated at the sides of the chancel (or platform, if the building is not a church). Participating clergy and lay persons will need places in the chancel or at the front of the congregation. Places will also be needed at the front of the congregation for the candidate and the lay and clerical presenters.

Sufficient communion stations to facilitate the communion of the people are prepared. One bread minister and two cup ministers will be needed at each. Sufficient vessels, including vessels that are large enough to consecrate the elements at the altar, will be needed.

A table or stand for the signing of the Declaration of Conformity with a copy of the declaration and a pen is placed near the bishop's chair. If a litany desk is used for the singing of the litany, it is placed at the front of the congregation.

The candidate's vestments and episcopal regalia need to be laid out in a place where they will be available conveniently when needed. Traditionally these are stole, chasuble, pectoral cross, mitre, ring, and pastoral staff. A

Bible to give to the new bishop is also needed. If they are to be blessed, this is done before the service (BCP 552).

A comprehensive service leaflet containing the entire service is almost essential for enabling participation. It will probably be impossible to have a proper rehearsal with all of the participants. It is helpful to have explicit written directions for each participant given to them before the service. A master of ceremonies (MC) who is familiar with all aspects of the service should be chosen. One or more assistant MCs to arrange particular parts of the service will be helpful.

Vesting space for the participating bishops and clergy and assembly space for lay persons participating in the service will be needed. The order and route of the entrance procession needs to be carefully worked out. If there will be more than one procession, an assistant MC takes charge of forming each procession.

The candidate is vested in a rochet or alb. The Presiding Bishop and the co-consecrators vest in alb, stole, chasuble (or cope), and mitre. The primatial cross may be carried before the Presiding Bishop by the chaplain. The concelebrating presbyters may wear alb, stole, and chasubles. The deacons reading the gospel and assisting at the altar may wear alb, stole, and dalmatic. Other presbyters and deacons may wear alb (or surplice) and stole. Participants, other than the newly ordained bishop, should not change vesture during the service. The changing of vestments during an ordination signifies the admission of the candidate, who arrives dressed in a white baptismal robe as a member of the people of God, to a new order signified by the vestments newly put on. The vestments are either red or white.

a. The Entrance and Presentation

The procession enters to the accompaniment of hymns, psalms, or anthems. The participants go to their places.

The Presiding Bishop, or another bishop appointed, says the opening acclamation and the collect for purity (BCP 512). It is preferable that this not be delegated, so that the one presiding is clearly identified.

The bishops and people sit. The bishops may wear their mitres. The candidate and the presenters come forward and stand before the Presiding Bishop. The presenters present the candidate, using the full name. The testimonials of election are then read. Those who read them come forward to a designated place to do so and then return to their places.

The bishop-elect makes the promise of conformity and then signs the declaration. The witnesses come forward and add their signatures.

The Presiding Bishop then asks the congregation for "any reason why we should not now proceed," and, if none is offered, asks the assent of the congregation and their prayers for the candidate (BCP 514). All kneel. The bishops remove their mitres and turn to kneel facing the altar, usually keeling against their chairs. The litanist goes to the litany desk, or other place appointed, and leads the Litany for Ordinations. It may be recited, but is usually sung. The music is in the Appendix to *The Hymnal 1982* at S 390.

The litany ends with the *Kyries* and the Presiding Bishop says or sings the salutation and the collect. Contrary to the normal practice, two collects may be used: the collect of the day and the collect for ordinations. When ordinations are held on major feasts, as is usually the case, the use of the collect of the day is most appropriate.

Following the collects, the candidate and the presenters return to their places. All sit.

b. The Ministry of the Word

Three lessons are always used. The Old Testament reading and the epistle are read by lay persons. The propers are selected by the Presiding Bishop from among those printed in the ordination rite, or, on Sundays or major feasts, from those of the day (BCP 515). "A psalm, canticle, or hymn follows each Reading" (BCP 516).

A deacon reads or sings the gospel in the usual manner. Although the rubric permits a priest to read the gospel, it is almost inconceivable that there will not be at least one deacon available to do so, and under no circumstances should a priest read the gospel if a deacon is a liturgical participant in the service.

The sermon follows the gospel. After the sermon a hymn is sung (BCP 516).

c. The Examination

All sit. The candidate stands facing the bishops. The Presiding Bishop puts on the mitre and begins the examination. The questions following may be asked by other bishops. After the candidate has responded to the final question, all stand, and the Presiding Bishop calls upon the bishop-elect to lead the Nicene Creed. The bishops remove their mitres.

d. The Consecration of the Bishop

The bishop-elect kneels before the Presiding Bishop. The other bishops stand to the left and right. The hymn *Veni Creator Spiritus* or *Veni Sancte Spiritus* is sung. Versions of *Veni Creator Spiritus* in *The Hymnal 1982* are "Come, Holy Ghost, our souls inspire" (Hymns 503, 504), "Creator Spirit, by whose aid" (Hymn 500), and "O Holy Spirit, by whose breath" (Hymns 501, 502). Versions of *Veni Sancte Spiritus* are "Come, thou Holy Spirit bright" (Hymns 226, 227), "Holy Spirit, font of light" (Hymn 228), and in *Wonder, Love, and Praise* the Taizé chant (Hymn 832). The prayer book no longer requires the hymn to be sung antiphonally with the bishop, and there is no reason to do so; probably the original intention of the rubric in 1550 was that the bishop precent the hymn by singing the opening line, and that it be sung antiphonally between choir and congregation. All stand in silent prayer.

The Presiding Bishop, standing and not wearing the mitre, begins the Prayer of Consecration with hands extended toward the candidate. At "Therefore, Father, make *N.* a bishop in your Church" the bishops lay their hands on the head of the bishop-elect, and recite the prayer together. At the place indicated in the prayer book, all remove their hands and the Presiding Bishop completes the prayer alone.

The bishops sit and put on their mitres. The presenters bring forward the vestments for the new bishop; they and other bishops may assist in the vesting. The new bishop is traditionally vested in stole, chasuble, and mitre. Although the pectoral cross is actually a symbol of office, not a vestment, it is more convenient if it is put on before the mitre.

The Bible is presented to the new bishop with the formula in the prayer book. The second part of the formula, "Feed the flock of Christ" (BCP 521), was originally intended to accompany the giving of the pastoral staff. This is sometimes done by the bishop's predecessor. The bishop may also be presented with a ring and any other appropriate symbols of office.

The Presiding Bishop presents the new bishop to the clergy and people for "their acclamation and applause." The new bishop greets the people with the peace. The bishops present greet the new bishop.

If the new bishop is the diocesan, and the service is in the cathedral, the bishop is now seated in the episcopal chair. The Presiding Bishop and the president of the Standing Committee escort the bishop to the *cathedra*. The dean of the cathedral meets the bishop at the chair and says:

In the name of *the Chapter* of this Cathedral Church, and on behalf of the people of this diocese, I install you, *N.*, in the chair appointed to your office. May the Lord stir up in you the flame of holy charity, and the power of faith that overcomes the world. *Amen.* (BOS 262)

e. The Eucharist

The liturgy then continues with the offertory. The new bishop is the chief celebrant, and other designated bishops and diocesan presbyters stand at the altar as concelebrants. The ordaining bishop and the principal co-consecrators will normally be included.

Deacons prepare the altar and stand on either side of the new bishop during the eucharistic prayer. One may assist with the book and the other with the elements. The bread and wine are brought to the altar by the family and friends of the new bishop (BCP 511).

The prayer book specifically states that the people shall be given opportunity to communicate. This is intended to forbid the practice of restricting the reception of communion to those in the sanctuary at large services, so sufficient ministers of communion and communion stations are necessary. The new bishop and some of the other bishops, presbyters, and deacons distribute communion.

After communion, the deacons and (if needed) priests take the remaining elements to the sacristy and reverently consume them.

One of the bishops leads the people in the special post-communion prayer (BCP 523). The new bishop and the concelebrants may remain at the altar or in their places.

The new bishop puts on the mitre, takes the pastoral staff, and goes to the center of the altar, either behind it or in front of it facing the people, if not already there. The new bishop blesses the people in the full pontifical form. The music is in *The Altar Book;* music for the responses is in *The Hymnal 1982* (S 173).

A deacon dismisses the people, and the exit procession forms. It usually goes down the center aisle. The newly ordained bishop, carrying the pastoral staff, if it was presented during the service, walks in front of the Presiding Bishop (and chaplain carrying the primatial cross) and of the diocesan bishop if the new bishop is a suffragan or coadjutor. The new bishop may be accompanied by deacons on each side.

The procession is appropriately accompanied by instrumental music and the ringing of church bells.

C. Recognition and Investiture of a Diocesan Bishop

The service in *The Book of Occasional Services* (BOS 253-259) is intended for use when a bishop previously ordained for another diocese becomes diocesan bishop. It is designed to be held in the cathedral. It can be adapted for use when a coadjutor or suffragan becomes diocesan, or in a building other than the cathedral.

> If a pastoral staff is used, it is carried by the former bishop in the welcoming procession, and presented to the new bishop at the time appointed. In the absence of the former bishop, it is placed on the Altar before the service begins. (BOS 252)

The Bible on which the oath will be taken is also placed upon the altar. The chair for the Presiding Bishop is placed at the entrance to the chancel.

The readings and psalm are selected from those appointed for the day, for the Ordination of a Bishop, or for Various Occasions (BOS 252).

The Presiding Bishop and the bishop are vested in alb, stole, cope, and mitre. The former bishop, if taking part in the investiture, may be similarly vested. The deacons wear alb, stole, and dalmatic. Other clerical participants may wear choir dress.

a. The Recognition

At the beginning of the service the choir, clergy, and other participants enter without ceremony. This and the welcoming procession's movement to the door may be accompanied by instrumental music. When all are in place, the Presiding Bishop, accompanied by a deacon, or two deacons, is escorted to the chair at the entrance of the chancel. The chaplain carrying the primatial cross may precede the Presiding Bishop. The deacons stand at the right and left of the chair.

A welcoming procession is formed to go to the door of the cathedral: a thurifer (if incense is used), crucifer with torchbearers left and right, representative clergy and laity of the diocese, the president of the Standing Committee (who acts as warden), and the former bishop (if present). The choir may form a part of the procession, or may remain in place to sing during the leading of the bishop through the nave of the cathedral.

The new bishop, attended by two deacons, comes to the door of the cathedral and, standing outside, knocks three times on the door. The warden opens the door. The bishop says, "Open for me the gates of righteousness; I will enter them and give thanks to the Lord." The warden replies, "The Lord prosper you: we wish you well in the Name of the Lord" (BOS 253).

A psalm or anthem is sung as the welcoming procession escorts the bishop through the congregation to a place before the Presiding Bishop. Psalm 23 is recommended, with the antiphon "I will give you a shepherd after my own heart, who will feed you with knowledge and understanding" (BOS 254).

Standing before the Presiding Bishop, the new bishop asks to be recognized and invested. The Presiding Bishop calls upon the warden to certify the election (BOS 254). The Presiding Bishop asks the people to recognize and uphold their bishop. When they assent, the Presiding Bishop asks for the people's prayers (BOS 255).

All kneel, and the Litany for Ordinations is sung as at ordinations. At the end of the litany, the Presiding Bishop sings (or says) the collect, either that of the day or of ordinations. "All sit, and the Liturgy of the Word continues in the usual manner" (BOS 255).

After the sermon (and the creed, if it is a part of the liturgy), the bishop renews the commitments of ordination. The bishop stands, without the mitre, before the Presiding Bishop, who sits in the chair. The dialogue takes place as provided in *The Book of Occasional Services* (BOS 255-257). The bishop puts on the mitre.

b. The Investiture

The Presiding Bishop stands and addresses the bishop as provided in *The Book of Occasional Services* (BOS 257). If the pastoral staff is to be given, the former bishop of the diocese presents it to the new bishop, saying:

On behalf of the people and clergy of the Diocese of _____, I give into your hands this pastoral staff. May Christ the good Shepherd uphold you and sustain you as you carry it in his name. *Amen.* (BOS 257)

If the former bishop is not present, the president of the Standing Committee takes the pastoral staff from the altar and presents it to the bishop, using the same words.

A deacon, or a diocesan officer, brings the Bible to the bishop, who lays a hand on it, and takes the oath (BOS 257).

c. The Seating

If the service is in the cathedral, the Presiding Bishop and president of the Standing Committee escort the bishop to the *cathedra*, as in the Ordination of Bishops above. The dean of the cathedral says the appointed form (BOS 258).

The bishop sits and the people applaud. Bells may be rung and trumpets sounded. The bishop greets the people with the peace, and the peace is exchanged, the Presiding Bishop and other ministers greeting the bishop.

d. The Eucharist

The eucharist continues with the offertory. The bishop presides as chief celebrant, while other bishops and representative priests of the diocese stand as concelebrants at the altar. The bishop may change the cope for the chasuble before going to the altar. Other concelebrants may put on chasubles. Deacons prepare the altar.

The bishop and as many other ministers as are necessary distribute communion to the clergy and people.

After communion one of the bishops or a priest leads the people in the special post-communion prayer from the Ordination of a Bishop (BCP 523, BOS 259).

The bishop gives the pontifical blessing, standing in the center of the altar, either behind it, or in front of it facing the people. The bishop wears the mitre and holds the pastoral staff in the left hand. The music is in *The Altar Book;* music for the responses is in *The Hymnal 1982* (S 173).

A deacon dismisses the people. The procession moves down the center aisle of the cathedral, as at the ordination of a bishop.

D. Welcoming and Seating of a Bishop in the Cathedral

This service is provided in *The Book of Occasional Services* (BOS 261-263) for use on the occasion of the bishop's first visit to the cathedral, if the ordination or investiture did not take place there.

If the service takes place on the same day as the ordination or investiture, there is no eucharist, and after the *Gloria in excelsis* or *Te Deum* the service concludes with the Lord's Prayer, the bishop's blessing, and the dismissal. Otherwise, the service is a celebration of the eucharist by the bishop.

The cathedral clergy and other representative persons go in procession to the cathedral door. The bishop, attended by two deacons and vested for the eucharist if it is to be celebrated, but otherwise in cope and mitre, stands before the cathedral door and knocks three times with the pastoral staff.

The appointed warden opens the door. The bishop enters and greets the congregation, "Grace and peace be with you, from God our Father and the Lord Jesus Christ." The people respond (BOS 261).

A psalm or anthem is sung as the bishop enters the cathedral. The procession halts at the front of the congregation or in some other place where the bishop is "in full sight of the people." The dean formally welcomes the bishop (BOS 261). The bishop responds. The bishop is escorted to the *cathedra* by the dean and the president of the Standing Committee (or other diocesan officer). The dean formally installs the bishop in the *cathedra* as in the previous services. The bishop sits and the people applaud. Bells may be rung and trumpets sounded (BOS 262).

The bishop stands and the *Te Deum, Gloria in excelsis,* or some other hymn of praise is sung. If there is no eucharist, the service concludes with the Lord's Prayer, the bishop's blessing, and the dismissal. Otherwise, the bishop continues the celebration of the eucharist with the collect. "At the Great Thanksgiving, the Bishop, as the principal Celebrant, is joined at the Altar by the presbyters of the Cathedral and other priests as desired" (BOS 263).

At the end of the service, the bishop gives the pontifical blessing, and a deacon dismisses the people.

Chapter Five

Liturgical Resources

Official Publications of the Episcopal Church

The following books are published by Church Publishing Corporation, New York:

- *The Book of Common Prayer* (1979)
  the prayer book of the Episcopal Church; revised in 1979
- *The Book of Occasional Services* (1994)
  revised every three years to include the actions taken at each General Convention
- *Lesser Feasts and Fasts* (1994)
  revised every three years to include the actions taken at each General Convention
- *The Altar Book*
  text and rubrics for the eucharistic liturgies of *The Book of Common Prayer*
- *Enriching our Worship* (1997)
  the successor to *Supplementary Liturgical Materials* (1994); prayers and liturgies in expansive language, approved by General Convention
- *The Hymnal 1982*
  includes service music and hymns
- *The Hymnal 1982, Accompaniment Edition*
  includes additional service music, harmonies, indicies, etc.
- *The Anglican Chant Psalter* (1987)
  the 150 psalms pointed for four-part Anglican chants
- *The Plainsong Psalter* (1988)
  the 150 psalms with antiphons, set to plainchant melodies

- *Gradual Psalms*
  in seven volumes; contains words and chants for psalms after the first reading, and Alleluias, tracts, and verses in use before the gospel
- *Musical Settings for Noonday and Compline*
  contains the full text and music for these offices as well as a selection of office hymns.
- *A New Metrical Psalter* (1986)
  contains metrical versions of the invitatories and canticles, and of those psalms used at the eucharist

Official Publications of the Anglican Church of Canada
The following books are published by the Anglican Book Centre, Toronto:
- *The Book of Alternative Services of the Anglican Church of Canada* (1985)
- *Occasional Celebrations of the Anglican Church of Canada* (1992)
- *For All the Saints: Prayers and Readings for Saints' Days According to the Calendar of the Book of Alternative Services of the Anglican Church of Canada* (1994)

Official Publications of the Church of England
- *The Promise of His Glory: Services and Prayers for the Season from All Saints to Candlemas.* Collegeville, Minn.: Liturgical Press, 1991.

Other Resources for Pastoral and Occasional Liturgies
- Associated Parishes. *Holy Baptism: A Liturgical and Pastoral Commentary.* Baltimore: Associated Parishes, 1997.
- Associated Parishes. *The Celebration and Blessing of a Marriage: A Liturgical and Pastoral Commentary.* Baltimore: Associated Parishes, 1996.
- Associated Parishes. *Holy Orders: The Ordination of Bishops, Priests, and Deacons.* Baltimore: Associated Parishes, 1991.
- Galley, Howard E. *The Ceremonies of the Eucharist: A Guide to Celebration.* Cambridge, Mass.: Cowley Publications, 1989.

- Galley, Howard E. *The Prayer Book Office.* New York: Church Hymnal Corporation, 1988.
- Hallenbeck, Edwin F., ed. *A Working Paper of Trial Liturgy for Celebration of Deacon's Ministry.* Providence, R. I.: North American Association for the Diaconate, 1996.
- Hyde, Clark. *To Declare God's Forgiveness: Toward a Pastoral Theology of Reconciliation.* Wilton, Conn.: Morehouse-Barlow, 1984.
- Melloh, John A., S. M., and William G. Storey, eds. *Praise God in Song: Ecumenical Daily Prayer.* Chicago: G. I. A. Publications, 1979.
- Mitchell, Leonel L. *Lent, Holy Week, Easter, and the Great Fifty Days: A Ceremonial Guide.* Cambridge, Mass.: Cowley Publications, 1996.
- Mitchell, Leonel L. *Praying Shapes Believing.* Harrisburg: Morehouse, 1991.
- Mitchell, Leonel L. *The Way We Pray.* Cincinnati: Forward Movement, 1984.
- Plater, Ormonde. *Intercession: A Theological and Practical Guide.* Cambridge, Mass.: Cowley Publications, 1995.
- Russell, Joseph P., ed. *The New Prayer Book Guide to Christian Education.* Cambridge, Mass.: Cowley Publications, 1996.
- Smith, Martin L., SSJE. *Reconciliation: Preparing for Confession in the Episcopal Church.* Cambridge, Mass.: Cowley Publications, 1985.
- Society of St. Francis. *Celebrating Common Prayer.* London: Mowbray, 1992.
- Stevick, Daniel. *Baptismal Moments, Baptismal Meanings.* New York: Church Hymnal Corporation, 1987.
- Stuhlman, Byron. *Occasions of Grace.* New York: Church Hymnal Corporation, 1996.
- Stuhlman, Byron. *Redeeming the Time.* New York: Church Hymnal Corporation, 1992.
- Taft, Robert. *The Liturgy of the Hours in East and West.* Collegeville, Minn.: Liturgical Press, 1986.
- Thurian, Max. *The Taizé Office.* London: Faith Press, 1966.
- Wright, J. Robert. *Readings for the Daily Office from the Early Church.* New York: Church Hymnal Corporation, 1991.